BUSINESS PRACTICE IN
THE COMMON MARKET

HEINZ COMMER

Business Practice in the Common Market

A Short Guide

FREDERICK A. PRAEGER, *PUBLISHER*
NEW YORK · LONDON

FREDERICK A. PRAEGER, *Publisher*

64 University Place, New York 3, N.Y., U.S.A.

49 Great Ormond Street, London WC1, England

Published in the United States of America in 1963
by Frederick A. Praeger, Inc., Publisher

Printed in Great Britain

PUBLISHER'S NOTE

Dr. Commer's book appeared in Germany in April 1962 and was specifically intended to be of help to German business men seeking to adjust to the new conditions of the Common Market. However, the scope of the book and the information it provides on current business practices in the Common Market give it more than a local relevance and make it a valuable handbook for all firms and individuals who have commercial dealings in EEC countries.

In certain points this English edition is different in structure from the German original. Information of an exclusively German relevance has in most cases been replaced by material of direct usefulness to British and American business men.

Introduction

The European Common Market has rightly been called the most important economic revolution of modern history. Its success is incontestable. The European market today is in the process of becoming a single market, but its effects are more far-reaching than a Customs Union. Since its transition to the second stage envisaged by the Rome Treaty, even sceptics have become convinced that integration is inevitable and will affect all enterprises whatever their size in all economic sectors. This is therefore an appropriate moment to review the experiences of the first four years of the European Common Market and to derive conclusions useful for business enterprise.

This book, based on actual experience and written principally for business men, describes events to date in the German Federal Republic and in other European countries, particularly in France, and discusses what further efforts are required.

It has been written solely to meet a practical need and is intended as a working tool for the business man. It establishes guiding principles, contains a short summary of basic data and describes practical experience. It includes only the most relevant matter and covers only present member states of the EEC. The outcome of current negotiations on new and Associate Members cannot be foreseen, but information applicable to existing partners of the Community will apply also to potential new members, subject to appropriate changes to an enlarged Community.

Many developments at present are only in their early stage. Nevertheless, business must prepare for changes now. The Common Market, with all its chances and risks, is growing irresistibly into an all-pervading influence.

Business men should not be discouraged by the problems of the Common Market. Much effort will be needed, but the well-established methods of business practice remain valid. Different languages are spoken in Europe; traditions of trade and thought processes differ. More specialised attention is required than in the more easily understood national market. This manual seeks to point out these requirements and to show how to meet them.

Special thanks are due to Dr. Albrecht Düren, Manager of the *Deutschen Industrie-und Handelstages,* and Dr. Roland Kuhn, Sector Chief of the DIHT, for their encouragement. My sincere thanks are due also to the Chambers of Industry and Commerce, as well as to many business men who have given me advice and help in writing this book.

One final word: various institutions are mentioned here as playing a part in the European market. Should any organisation not be mentioned, I would like to apologise for this oversight. I would be grateful for any information which could be utilised in future editions.

HEINZ COMMER

Analysis of Contents

Part IV: Retrospect and Prospect

Appendices

PART I

GUIDE FOR A PRACTICAL BUSINESS POLICY IN THE EUROPEAN MARKET

A Twelve-Point Program

Summary of the Program

All departments of firms must adjust themselves to the requirements of the European Common Market. Essential points in the program recommended for them to follow are:

I   Information: utilisation of all international and national sources of information on the European Common Market.

II   Improving economic, business, demographic and ethnographic knowledge.

III   Furthering the knowledge of languages by employees, using suitable means within as well as outside the firm.

IV   Marketing in the Common Market: market research, motivation research, advertising, public relations, adjustment of sales and buying to new conditions.

V   Adjustment to the competitive position of the European market: tariffs, locality, standards and comparison with competitors' products.

VI   Co-operation between firms, inter-firm comparisons, licences.

VII   Improving internal information on EEC matters as an aspect of adjustment to European integration.

VIII   Examination of program planning: specialisation in and reduction of product range.

IX   Utilisation of the credit possibilities arising from the Common Market Treaty.

X   Investigation of labour-market problems: observing European labour markets; the welfare of foreign employees.

XI   Adjusting basic and further vocational training to the requirements of the integrated European market.

XII   Co-operation with Chambers of Industry and Commerce and other associations.

GUIDE FOR A PRACTICAL BUSINESS POLICY

Point One
Utilising Sources of General Information

Information comes before action in the European market. European industrial integration has been fashionable for the last ten years and has encouraged a vast output particularly of theoretical literature. As this book is designed for practical application, only the most important written sources are mentioned and in this translation mainly British sources are quoted. References to specialist literature are included in the respective individual sections.

This section surveys the most important literature sources. Books which have now become standard literature are:

Britain and Europe: The Economist Intelligence Unit.

The Community of Europe: Richard Mayne: Gollancz.

The Common Market—Its Structure and Purpose: J. F. Deniau: Barrie & Rockliff, with Pall Mall Press. Published in the United States by Frederick A. Praeger.

The Challenge of the Common Market: U. W. Kitzinger: Blackwell. Published in the United States by Frederick A. Praeger.

Appendix IX lists and discusses these and other books and pamphlets on the Common Market published in Britain and the United States.

The most important sources in addition to the specialised literature mentioned in the individual sections are the following:

A. INTERNATIONAL SOURCES

I PUBLICATIONS BY THE EEC ORGANISATIONS
(Council of Ministers and the Commission)

Official publications of the European Common Market organisations, for example EEC Regulations and the *Official*

Journal of the European Communities, are obtainable in Britain through Her Majesty's Stationery Office. The information service of the European Communities, 23 Chesham Street, London, S.W.1, has also available a wide range of publications. The statistics published by the Statistical Office of the European Communities, the Annual Reports, as well as individual studies on social policy and regional development, are of great importance. In the United States, official publications are obtainable from the Superintendent of Documents, Government Printing Office, Washington 25, D.C., and from the European Community Information Service, Suite 808, the Farragut Building, Washington 6, D.C.

II PUBLICATIONS BY THE EUROPEAN PARLIAMENT

The detailed *Quarterly Bibliography* published by the Department for Parliamentary Documentation and Information of the European Parliament in Luxemburg deserves special mention.

The same organisation lists in *Europa-Dokumentation* publications of individual Governments, professional organisations and literature dealing with special problems of European integration.

III PUBLICATIONS BY THE EFTA SECRETARIAT

The general Secretariat of EFTA publishes the EFTA Bulletin obtainable from the General Secretary of EFTA, rue des Colombettes, Geneva, Switzerland.

B NATIONAL SOURCES

I LAWS AND REGULATIONS

Business men naturally are particularly interested in publications of laws and regulations. The title and source of these publications in those European countries which are either members or have applied for membership or associate membership of the EEC are listed below.

	Title of Publication	*Address*
BELGIUM	*Moniteur Belge*	40–42, rue Louvain, Brussels 1
DENMARK	*Lovtidende for Kongeriget Danmark Teil A—C*	J. H. Schultz A/S, Copenhagen
EEC	*Official Journal of the European Communities*	Her Majesty's Stationery Office, Kingsway, London, W.C.2
FRANCE	*Journal Officiel de la République Française, Lois et décrets*	Imprimerie des Journaux Officiels, 26, rue Desaix, Paris
GREECE	*Efimeristis kywerniseos*	EthnikonTypografeion Kapodistriou 34, Athens

BRITAIN

In Great Britain all laws, decrees, and regulations are published as individual documents and not within a regularly appearing series
Her Majesty's Stationery Office, York House, Kingsway, London, W.C.2

IRELAND

In Ireland all laws, decrees and regulations are published as individual documents and not within a regularly appearing series
Government Publications Sale Office, G.P.O. Arcade, Dublin

| ITALY | *Gazzetta Ufficiale della Repubblica Italiana* | Istituto Poligrafico dello stato—Libreria dello stato Piazza G. Verdi 10, Rome |

LUXEMBURG	*Mémorial Journal Officiel du Grand-Duché de Luxembourg A. Recueil de législation*	Imprimerie de la Cour Victor Buck, S.e.c.s. Luxemburg
NETHERLANDS	*Staatsblad van het Koninkrijk der Nederlanden*	Staatsdrukkerij uitgeverijbedrijf, Fluwelen Burgwall 18, The Hague
NORWAY	*Norsk Lovtidend*	Grondahl & Sohn, Oslo
AUSTRIA	*Bundesgesetzblatt für die Republik Österreich*	Verkaufsstelle der Österreichischen Staatsdruckerei, Wollzeile 27a, Vienna 1
SWEDEN	*Svenska Författningssamling*	Kungl, Boktryckeriet P.A. Norstedt & Söner, Stockholm
SWITZERLAND	*Bundesblatt der schweizerischen Eidgenossenschaft*	Stämpfli & Cie, Hallstr. 7, Bern
	Schweizerisches Handelsamtsblatt	Handelsabteilung des Eidgenössischen Volkswirtschaftsdepartementes, Effingerstr. 3, Bern

II OFFICIAL TRADE INFORMATION IN WEST GERMANY

The *Bundesstelle für Aussenhandels-information* (BfA) at Blenbreck 13, Cologne, publishes, within the framework of its market information service, economics reports, particularly on EEC and EFTA countries. Business organisations and individual firms may obtain these without cost. The BfA now publishes also the *Europa Dokumentation*, a quarterly which lists all publications on European integration, the overall development of individual European national economies and their respective sectors. Collected information on adjustment measures by firms in European countries is published every two months. In addition the statistical sources for market research purposes are gradually being listed.

Europa Dokumentation is available to German business organisations and firms without cost.

III OFFICIAL TRADE INFORMATION IN BRITAIN AND THE UNITED STATES

In Britain, HMSO issues a monthly list of government publications. These publications include not only documents originating from government departments and other public authorities, but also from the European Community and EFTA and other national bodies. The Board of Trade Journal, published weekly, is particularly informative with regard to trade information. Similar lists, bibliographies and publications are available in the United States from the Superintendent of Documents, Government Printing Office.

IV PERIODICALS AND INFORMATION SERVICES

The Chambers of Industry and Commerce are useful sources of information. The International Chamber of Commerce, 38 Cours Albert I-er Paris VIII, publishes a number of valuable brochures and documents on international and European trade, available in the United States through the U.S. Council of the I.C.C., 103 Park Avenue, New York.

In Britain, periodical publications include:

Marketing in Europe: a monthly series published by the Economist Intelligence Unit.

Europe: daily reports published by the Agence Internationale d'Information pour la Presse, Luxembourg. (In English.)

Common Market News: weekly news bulletin published by Comtel-Reuter. (In English.)

Eurotariff: gives information of all changes in duties and classifications for all commodities.

Business in Europe: published weekly by Business International, Geneva. (In English.)

Journal of Common Market Studies: published three times a year by Blackwell.

In America, periodicals (in addition to those listed above) include *International Commerce*, published by the U.S Department of Commerce; *Report on Western Europe*, published by the Chase Manhattan Bank, New York; *Bulletin from the European Community*, published by the European Community Information service; and *Commerce Business Daily*, published by the Department of Commerce.

Point Two

Improving Economic, Business, Demographic and Ethnographic Knowledge of EEC Countries

To meet business requirements in the Common Market, it is not necessary to possess highly detailed information about other European countries. The business man must be aware, however, of the relative position of their subsidiaries or agents within the economy of the EEC countries. The statistical year books issued by individual Common Market countries are valuable sources of material. These statistical year books and also the statistics published by the Joint Statistical Office of the European Communities show, amongst other useful information, the age distribution in Common Market countries. The importance to business men of age distribution or population statistics requires no emphasising. It forms the basis for business planning—marketing, distribution of potential buyers, etc. These data affect also the recruitment policy for potential managers and their training.

Income statistics of potential buyers are important in relation to price policy. Some firms already possess such demographic data; others should follow their example.

A. RELEVANT DATA

In addition to information on the economies of Europe, the following data is worth obtaining in relevant cases:

Climatic conditions
Average body size
Average body weight
Average hand and foot size
Mode of living
Users' habits
Moral laws (influence on dress requirements)

Relative importance of consumer preferences (e.g. relative
preference for food, clothing or housing)
Trade mark requirements
Laws affecting food
Preferences or dislikes (for example, of colour, or in relation
to particular groups or localities, also "taboos" of various
kinds).

B. SOURCES OF OFFICIAL STATISTICS

The addresses of the statistical offices and the title of the
statistical year books in Common Market countries are listed
below:

	Office	*Title of Statistical Year Book*
BELGIUM	Institut National de Statistique, 44, rue de Louvain, Brussels	*Annuaire Statistique de la Belgique*
FRANCE	Institut National de la Statistique et des Etudes Economiques pour la Métropole et la France d'Outre-Mer (INSEE), 29, quai Branly, Paris 7e	*Annuaire Statistique France*
ITALY	Instituto Centrale di Statistica Via Cesare Balbo, 16, Rome	*Annuario statistico italiano*
LUXEMBURG	Office de la Statistique Générale, 19, avenue de la Porte-Neuve, Luxemburg	*Annuaire Statistique*
NETHERLANDS	Centraalbüro voor de Statistiek Oostduin-laan 2, The Hague	*Statistisch Zakboek*

	Office	Title of Statistical Year Book
EUROPEAN COMMUNITY	Statistical Office of the European Community, 118a, avenue de Tervueren, Brussels 15	*Bulletin of Statistics*
WEST GERMANY	Statistisches Bundesamt Gustav-Stresemann-Ring 11, Wiesbaden	*Statistisches Jahrbuch*

C. NOMENCLATURE AND LEGAL BASIS OF BUSINESS ORGANISATIONS

The types of business organisations in Common Market countries should be known. Differing regulations affecting business organisations in individual Common Market countries may be of significance. The main types of business organisations, with their legal nomenclature, are as follows:

	Classification	Approximate English Equivalent
BELGIUM	Société anonyme	Joint stock company
	Société en nom collectif	Private company
	Société en commandite simple	Limited partnership
	Société en commandite par actions	Partnership limited by shares
	Société des personnes à responsabilité limité	Private limited liability company
	Société coopérative	Co-operative Society
	Union de crédit	Loan Society

	Classification	Approximate English Equivalent
FRANCE	Société anonyme	Joint stock company
	Société en nom collectif	Private company
	Société en commandite simple	Limited partnership
	Société en commandite par actions	Partnership limited by shares
	Société à responsabilité	Private limited liability company
	Société à capital variable	Company with variable capital
ITALY	Società per azioni	Joint stock company
	Società in nome collettivo	Private company
	Società in accomandita semplice	Limited partnership
	Società in accomandita per azioni	Partnership limited by shares
	Società a responsabilità limitata	Private limited liability company

In addition, co-operatives and mutual insurance societies exist in Italy. "Sleeping partnerships" are less frequent.

NETHERLANDS	Naamlooze Venootschap (N.V.)	Joint stock company
	Venootschap onder een Firma	Private company
	Venootschaphij wijse van Geldschieting	Limited partnership

Private limited liability companies are not known in the Netherlands.

WEST GERMANY	Aktien Gesellschaft (A.G.)	Public company
	Offene Handelsgesellschaft (O.H.G.)	Partnership

	Classification	Approximate English Equivalent
WEST GERMANY *ctd.*	Kommandit-Gesellschaft (K.G.)	Limited partnership
	Kommandit-Gesellschaft auf Aktien (K.G.a.A.)	Company limited by shares having one or more general partners
	Gesellschaft mit beschränkter Haftung (GmbH)	Limited liability company
	Genossenschaft	Co-operative association
	Kreditverein	Credit union

Note: The legal basis of company organisation varies from country to country and the translation represents the nearest, but not necessarily the exact, equivalent in Britain.

Knowledge about business organisations is required particularly when considering close co-operation with outside firms. Loose partnerships are one possibility; others are investing in existing firms or establishing a new firm in association with a local business. Even when establishing subsidiaries some knowledge of organisation form is essential.

Ethnographic knowledge of the Common Market is also of great importance. For example, a German firm not long ago distributed sales literature written in French in the Flemish provinces of Belgium. The reaction of the Flemish nationalists was certainly not the one intended! Hostility to an advertisement considered offensive became associated with the firm offering the products, so that the sales effort proved unsatisfactory. Civil engineering firms who set up their site-advertisements in the French language in Flanders did not establish a desirable public image.

Point Three

Improving Knowledge of Languages

The common internal market of the United States and the European Common Market are frequently compared and there is reasonable hope that the six will achieve a full integration of their economies similar to that of the United States. Nevertheless the European Common Market differs from the American market in that differing languages are spoken.

A. INCREASED IMPORTANCE OF LANGUAGES IN INTERNAL EEC TRADE

The consequences of the Common Market for the business man are as follows:

At present, firms operate in a national market. By 31st December 1969 at the latest, firms will operate within a Common Market. Adaptation to the changing markets in supply, sales, capital and labour requires business men to be familiar with the languages of the Common Market to a much greater extent than hitherto. French is particularly important as it is the foremost social and business language in the three Benelux countries and Italy. English might catch up in importance with French should Britain and other EFTA countries join the Community or become Associated Members.

Some business men have recently stressed that sales representatives become fully effective in the Common Market only when their knowledge, for example of French, is such that they can evaluate advertisements and other sales-material. Foreign languages are important also in many fields: in discussions, in correspondence, labelling, prospectuses and various other advertising media. Unfortunately, it is no longer customary to send young business men for their training to foreign countries. This is surprising considering that broad sectors of the population can now afford to visit foreign countries and that international activities and youth exchanges have become very popular.

Here is an example, typical of German indifference in this matter. At the Trade Fair at Salonika in Greece (an Associate Member of the EEC) the German sales-effort was conducted exclusively in the German language. Everyone who knew anything about Greece prophesied that potential sales would suffer. And they did. Potential sales to the value of millions were lost.

Knowledge of languages is of even greater importance in trading with countries which are members of the Community. It has been suggested recently that trade marks and product-characterisation should be evaluated with a view to their effectiveness throughout Europe. The names and publicity presentation—the "image"—of firms might be so formulated as to be attractive to clients and customers in other European countries. The possibility of Europeanising the names of firms should be examined, and attention given to considering the feasibility of forming trade marks or business names by a combination of Germanic and Latin syllables.

Language is also important in furthering communication between a firm and the offices of the European Communities and other European organisations. In translating specific words, it is sometimes very difficult to establish the corresponding meaning in another language. Special technical expressions frequently cannot be translated at all. To establish a common denominator, the publications of the organisations of the EEC are employing expressions which are current in French or English. For example, the word *Indikation*, which in German is used only in mathematics, has become absorbed via the French language into Common Market jargon as *indication*. It now means, in Brussels usage, something like "a certain factor". Such new terminologies are not the result of failure on the part of translators, but a necessary improvisation. A knowledge of French and English is therefore essential. The writer hopes he will be forgiven for referring to his own publication: the *European Common Market Dictionary* (published by Erich Schmidt Verlag Berlin, Bielefeld, Munich). This reference is necessary since no other specific EEC dictionary is as yet available.

It does little good simply to complain about the deplorable situation in regard to the use, or rather misuse, of foreign languages in the export trade, or to engage in detailed considera-tion of the reasons for it. It is much more important to concentrate on improving the situation. German diplomatic and commercial missions in foreign countries are working on the right lines, for example, in following up individual cases and in seeking to convert the "offending firm". The German Chambers of Com-merce also are to be congratulated on their bringing home to firms the importance of good translations. Faulty translations and their numerous examples of *gaucherie* are a source of ridicule, particularly in South America. Hoped-for business is not the least of the casualties caused by such ridicule.

In the long run, however, the problem can only be solved by sound, intensive and prolonged training of the business man and his associates in the most important foreign languages. This training should not be left to the private initiative of the individual. It is cheaper in the long run for firms to provide the time and money for such training than to wait in the hope that someone good at languages (and generally highly paid) will turn up on their staff.

B. MEANS OF TRAINING IN LANGUAGES

What are the best means of training in languages? The following methods are practicable.

I WITHIN THE FIRM

Language courses may be arranged which are open to em-ployees either at little or at no cost. Further, personal contact can be encouraged between employees in both domestic and foreign industry, either during or out of working time. Govern-ment departments and major commercial organisations have already acted on these lines and have established language courses. Generally speaking, however, language courses within firms are possible only for large organisations.

Making available foreign newspapers and journals to those interested is always useful. Encouraging personnel exchange is also important from the language point of view.

II OUTSIDE THE FIRM

The following possibilities arise for encouraging employees to study languages:

  (i) Paying for the cost of courses, for example at technical schools and other institutes of further education, such as business and language schools.

 (ii) Paying for holiday courses in foreign and particularly in EEC universities.

Apart from these direct methods, endeavours to strengthen and improve knowledge of languages will only be successful if those who so equip themselves are suitably rewarded. Suitable rewards may take the form of wage or salary increases, preference in employment and career opportunities, together with due recognition being given to language-qualifications in personal records and so forth.

Business men who do not themselves speak foreign languages sometimes say that translating or even interpreting is a second- or third-class occupation. This is certainly not true. A good interpreter has to be an expert in his own field and in addition must have a "feeling" for languages. He requires many years of training and a natural talent for sensing the inner meaning of the speaker or writer. One cannot too strongly censure the practice of giving the job of translating to those who have only a limited knowledge of languages. This is a self-defeating and deleterious policy. Every business man should remember the saying that the best case has little prospect of success if defended by an incompetent lawyer. Equally the most favourable offer loses its power of persuasion when presented in an incomprehensible language due to poor translation.

Point Four

Marketing in the Common Market

Marketing is successful when there has been proper co-ordination of research, product development, sales organisation and effort, and good public relations. In local markets there may well be some scope for business instincts: in the wider European area, however, it is better to base activity on an extensive knowledge of the market. Right from the start, a thorough study of the market is desirable.

A. MARKET INVESTIGATION

The chief sources of competition abroad are: competition from other Common Market countries; competition from non-EEC countries (the growing pressure from the USA is particularly noteworthy); and local competition. The changing competitive situation requires constant study. For this purpose, the services of either national or perhaps European market research organisations should be utilised. In Western Germany, the Federal Office for Foreign Trade Information (in its valuable publication *Wirtschaftliche Informations—und Dokumentationsstellen in den Ländern der Europäischen Wirtschaftsgemeinschaft*) lists in detail the various possibilities. In Britain, the Board of Trade is a valuable source of information on trading opportunities in other countries.

Frequently market research is looked on as being primarily *sales research*. This, however, is too narrow an attitude. More relevant is the formula put forward by Professor Dr. Hans A. Münster, with the Common Market specifically in mind:

> "Market research is the systematic investigation of the total production, distribution and consumption process within the Common Market in general, and in particular in every state and in all its respective economic sectors, as well as individual investigations in these states."

I MARKET RESEARCH

Before deciding on a market research investigation, consideration should be given to the following outline by Professor Dr. Erich Schafer in his book *Grundlage der Marktforschung* (Basic Principles of Market Research), third edition Cologne and Opladen, 1953:

1. A clear formulation of the purpose of the investigation. (Why do we need the investigation?)

2. Scope of the investigation. (What do we require to know for this purpose? What factors should be established or clarified?)

3. Sources of information. (Who can supply this information, divided according to user, trader, etc.; locality, town, country, etc.; and numbers to be questioned?)

4. Organisation of plan of investigation. (By whom should the data be collected? Internal or outside research organisations? What type of personnel is required, what should be its cost and who is to exercise control?)

5. Planning of the investigation. (What form should the investigation take—oral, written, by means of questionnaires, etc.?)

6. Sample investigation, followed, if necessary, by revision of the existing plan.

After deciding on the overall plan of the investigation, one comes to the detailed approach to the survey. Who should carry out the investigation is the first point to be determined. The firm itself, or its relevant department, is one possibility. In most cases, however, this is not desirable. Even the largest organisations do not carry out their own surveys. They draw up the required questionnaires, guide and observe the preparation and execution of the survey, but it is their general practice to entrust the actual investigation to market research organisations.

These latter co-operate with corresponding organisations abroad.

In Britain there are many companies which undertake market research. Some are subsidiaries of advertising agencies while others are independent. The Market Research Society, 39 Hertford Street, London, W.1., is their main representative organisation.

To reduce costs the survey should be carried out whenever possible in three phases:

1. Investigation of the general economic position of the relevant economy or area, *i.e.* basic data on economics and trade.

2. Investigation of the sales potential of the firm's product within a predetermined area (the market situation).

3. Investigation of relevant individual factors, *e.g.* packing, advertising and distribution.

Such a step-by-step approach makes it easier to discontinue the project should the results during the early part of the survey prove unsatisfactory.

A number of publications deal with market research:

In Britain, the Market Research Society produces its own *Journal*.

In the United States, the American Marketing Association (East Monroe Street, Chicago 3, Ill.) publishes the *Journal of Marketing*.

France is very active in market research. Several institutes have been founded in France during the last three years; intended for the purposes of private industry, they are nevertheless supported by the state. For example, two years ago a French private firm carried out a market investigation in an important German port and was actively assisted by the French consulate. To give an example of the French method: a French market research institute used large numbers of interviewers in a thorough investigation of whole areas in order to obtain data on the purchasing habits of consumers and on the sales potential of the products of the French foodstuff industry. Data were obtained also on possible direct sales to potential purchasers.

II MOTIVATION RESEARCH

Motivation research may be desirable when introducing a new product to another EEC country. Data should be obtained on the motives which sway potential purchasers when buying a specific product; on their reasons for selecting one product and rejecting others; and on the desires of the public as a whole. Such information is particularly important with respect to product design and to the organisation of the sales effort. Dr. Ernst Dichter, the Manager of the Institute for Motivation Research, Croton Hill, USA, is an acknowledged expert on this subject, which involves the use of psycho-analytical techniques in marketing. He suggests that the following factors should be considered when introducing a new product:

1. Highest possible quality of form and substance.

2. Originality, if possible unique characterisation: "Nothing like this has ever been known before!"

3. Reference to tradition, and, in certain circumstances, stress on the country of origin. (Americans favour French perfume, even when produced in America under a French name.)

Motivation research in a specific country may supply data on:

(i) Those characteristics of the product which act positively (*i.e.* encourage the purchaser), and those which act negatively (*i.e.* discourage him).

(ii) Required characteristics of a new product to maximise sales potential.

(iii) Motives favourable to the product which could be mobilised by packaging and sales effort.

To quote from an article in *Weltwoche* by Dr. Dichter:

"In Italy we are at present carrying out an investigation into the reaction of the Italian housewife to pre-cooked tinned food. In Germany we have a cigarette manufacturer as a client. In London and Paris our branch organisations work for bakeries, a car manufacturer and a ladies' clothing concern. We are dealing also with problems of the Common Market. Regarding the European Common Market, the main difficulties are not economic, but psychological. One has to take account of many prejudices."

Motivation research may, of course, also be carried through by a home-based market research organisation.

B. SALES EFFORT

United States experience shows the tremendous importance of sales effort in a large market. Sales promotion will grow substantially within the EEC. Calculations indicate that taking account of the existing known factors, sales promotion effort in Europe is likely to increase by at least 50 per cent during the next five years. The countries which to date have lagged in sales promotion will probably make a special effort. This is particularly true of Italy. For the year 1960 the Federal Republic shows a relatively high sales promotion effort per head of the population. Federal Republic: *DM 81;* Belgium and Luxemburg: *DM 45*; Netherlands: *DM 42*; France: *DM 33*; and Italy: *DM 12*.

Which are the most important factors in increasing sales effort? First of all, experience in the home market. It is, however, important to appreciate that many factors differ in other EEC countries. Four different languages are spoken, income and consequently purchasing power differ sharply, and purchasing requirements differ in relation to different sociological structures. The temperament and living habits of Italians differ from those of Germans or Belgians. Demand differs for type, quality and presentation of product. Market and motivation research are frequently the only means of obtaining adequate information on these matters.

A great deal depends initially on how well the firm is known in the new market, on whether a specialised product is offered which is of interest only to a few purchasers (investment product), or whether sales are sought from a large number of purchasers (consumer products). All further steps depend on these factors.

The market, and the organisation of sales therein, may justify a special sales department. It may, however, be practicable to use agents within the country. But in either case the planning of the sales effort should be done in the country concerned and should not be introduced from outside. At the same time, the exporter must obtain information on how sales and promotion are organised in individual countries, on the services obtainable from agents for specified fees, and on current price structure and discounts.

I ADVERTISING

The method of selling goods to purchasers determines to a large extent the approach to the sales effort. Not all the advertising media available in the home market are available in other EEC countries. In Italy, television and radio advertising has only recently come into use. In some countries, sales representatives are substantially more important than in, say, Western Germany. With regard to press advertisements, it should be noted that in the Latin countries insertions are arranged by agents and factors, whereas in Germany space is usually offered directly by the journals themselves.

Of comparable importance in sales effort are:

1. Sales discussion, mainly by representatives.

2. Sales literature, brochures, catalogues, sales journals, names of firms in shop windows, on delivery vans, packaging.

3. Fairs and exhibitions.

4. Sales films, photographs.

5. Several radio and television stations.

Advertisement by aeroplane is appropriate to some firms.

The *International Media Guide* publishes yearly lists and rates on all media throughout the Western world with the exception of the United States and Canada. The Guide includes information on newspapers, magazines, radio, outdoor and cinema advertising.

(a) LEADING EUROPEAN NEWSPAPERS AND PERIODICALS

Leading newspapers in 17 European countries accept advertisements within the framework of the international *Top European Advertising Media* (TEAM). The papers taking part cover a wide readership. The figures in brackets indicate circulation.

BELGIUM: *Le Soir* (301,285); *Het laatste Nieuws* (288,259); DENMARK: *Berlingske Tidende* (185,363); GERMANY: *Frankfurter Allgemeine Zeitung* (225,114), *Die Welt* (228,203), *Süddeutsche Zeitung* (221,289); FRANCE: *Le Figaro* (465,931), *Le Monde* (221,412); BRITAIN: *The Guardian* (212,263); NORWAY: *Aftenposten* (168,334); ITALY: *Corriere della Sera* (460,000), *Il Messaggero* (250,000); NETHERLANDS: *Algemeen Handelsblad* (62,000), *Nieuwe Rotterdamse Courant* (51,702); AUSTRIA: *Die Presse* (52,000); SWEDEN: *Svenska Dagbladet* (136,532); SWITZERLAND: *Neue Zürcher Zeitung* (73,320).

Leading business papers form another group. These are known as the *Top 5 Group*: FRANCE: *La Vie Française*; BELGIUM: *La Metropole*; NETHERLANDS: *Elseviers Wegblad*; ITALY: *24 Ore*; GERMANY: *Handelsblatt*.

Other leading periodicals of international repute include, in Germany: *Die Zeit, Rheinischer Merkur, Christ und Welt,* together with the business papers *Industriekurier* and *Der Volkswirt*; and in Britain: *The Financial Times* (a daily) and *The Economist*. Whether advertising in these papers is worthwhile depends on the market the advertiser is aiming at. Potential purchasers of widely used consumer goods can be contacted better through a newspaper having a wide circulation than through a specialised business paper.

The International Chamber of Commerce has published in English and French a manual on *Advertising: Conditions and Regulations in Various Countries*, which outlines regulations and conditions in fourteen countries.

(b) FACTORS IN ADVERTISING

The relative importance of advertising media differs greatly from country to country. Accordingly an exact knowledge of sales and advertising habits of the potential market is required. This implies awareness and continuous observation of the methods of local competitors. Whether exporters should use an approach similar to that employed by local competitors, or a distinctive one to stress differences, depends on opportunity and skill.

No firm can hope to conquer a whole country for all its products immediately. Apart from other factors, its resources would scarcely be adequate for such a task. At first one should concentrate on the most promising products and, in addition, on a specific area (town, province or homogeneous economic region).

Potential purchasers should always be addressed in their own language. This may be difficult sometimes, for example, in Belgium unless the precise whereabouts of the language frontier between the Flemish and French-speaking population is known. A German manufacturer was strongly criticised by the local press when he advertised in French for labour within the Flemish-speaking districts.

The appropriate language must be used correctly. Consequently all texts should be checked and if necessary altered within each country to which goods are sent.

Statements are effective only when using the right psychological stress either in picture or text. National, religious or aesthetic feelings may be offended through inappropriate pictures or through false selection of colours (national colours). Colour used in sales literature is of considerable importance.

Permanent success whether at home or abroad can be built only on the basis of truth, clarity and sales effectiveness. Some such slogan as "Be different—be you!" or "Strike out on your own" can be valuable in showing the special characteristics of the product offered. Repetition is equally necessary.

Finally the exporter should be aware of the laws and regulations determining sales promotion in overseas markets. The laws governing competition and advertising differ substantially as between countries. Differences occur particularly with regard to advertisements comparing products. These are forbidden in West Germany but not necessarily elsewhere. Differences occur also in regulations on medical products, food products and others.

Small firms can establish a good position in the Common Market by co-operating with other firms, or by launching a sales drive for a complete individual trading or industrial sector. Such means have been used successfully in the home market, for example, by the textile industry, the brewing industry, etc. A further field for co-operation lies in joint exhibitions covering whole sectors of industry in trade fairs abroad.

(c) MARKET RESEARCH AND ADVERTISING ORGANISATIONS

The leading market research and advertising organisations in the six EEC countries have established a common organisation, the *Communauté Européenne des Organisations Publicitaires* (CEOP), which seeks to improve the organisational/legal basis of advertising and sales promotion. The CEOP runs expert committees on sales, agents, representatives, the press, posters, cinema, radio and television. In addition, there is the European Association of Advertising Agencies (EAAA) (Peter Str. 1, Zürich), the European Direct Mail Association (Spital Str. 2, Basle), the *Socéité Française d'Affichage Routier* (65 rue de la Victoire, Paris) and the *Fédération Française de la Publicité* (27 *bis* Avenue de Villiers, Paris 17e).

II GUIDING PRINCIPLES OF SALES PROMOTION

The activities of the above-mentioned organisations are vital and outstandingly valuable in that they can do the groundwork for firms. But, ultimately, sales depend on the firm's own initiative.

All sales promotion should take account of the following scheme, the main elements of which appear to have general application:

1. *Sales plan containing data on:*
   - (a) area,
   - (b) time (season),
   - (c) volume.

2. *Data on potential market:*
   - (a) climatic conditions within the sales area,
   - (b) general attitudes of potential customers,
   - (c) living habits,
   - (d) purchasing habits.

3. *Data on relevant authorities at home and abroad dealing with foreign trade and sales promotion.*

4. *Data on the advertising media to be used.*

5. *Timing of the sales effort.*

Experience to date within the Common Market has shown the worth of one particular method which has been effectively employed in the German market by firms from other EEC countries, namely, approaching the customer as a partner, a colleague, as a fellow-passenger in the good ship *Europa*. The customer or client is accordingly addressed as "Common Market friend" (*EWG-Freund*), an approach which has proved highly successful in sales promotion in Germany.

The following examples are instructive:

1. A French producer of chocolates advertised French "cat tongues" from Paris as follows: "In anticipation

of customs reductions—enjoy now all advantages of the European Common Market." "Through high productivity to the new EEC bargain price."

2. A German Bank stressed the many new opportunities available to the German export trade due to the European Common Market and other reductions in custom tariffs. Appropriate business connections, however, needed to be established. The Bank pointed to its widespread network of representatives and declared its readiness to establish connections between clients and interested trading partners in the Common Market and in other countries.

These examples and many others show that imagination is necessary to conquer essential European markets. The merit of EEC is that it greatly facilitates the process.

C. PUBLIC RELATIONS

The importance of public relations has increased in line with sales effort in Europe. In his particularly instructive book on the European Market: *Public Relations als unternehmerische Aufgabe in der neuen und alten Welt* (Industrie-Verlag Carlheinz Gehlsen GmbH., Heidelberg and Berlin), Adalbert Schmidt interprets the concepts of public relations as including all planned considerations and efforts which facilitate understanding between a firm or an institution and the public, and which create and maintain mutual confidence. This implies, with regard to the European Market, that all possible means should be used by the firm to explain to the European public the reasons for its existence and activity; clearly a difficult and time-consuming task. A step-by-step process is therefore advisable, by selecting in the first instance, just as in sales promotion, those areas which are of particular importance to the firm. In these the public image of the firm should be established with public and local authorities, the population and, more particularly, the potential purchasers.

Many approaches are possible in public relations. Only the more important are shown here by way of example.

1. *Public relations advertisements* (in contrast to sales advertisements which seek to encourage a purchase, public relations advertisements seek to establish an identification and a thought-association between the reader and the firm).

2. *Effective publicity of annual general meetings in newspaper articles and house-publications.*

3. *Contacts with the press* (popularised data on "jubilees" of the firm and on other suitable occasions).

4. *Contacts with the public* (visits to the firm).

5. *Films about the firm* (feature-films for cinema or television).

Public relations should underline that the firm as a whole, and not only its sales sector, can be of value and interest to the public. A good public relations campaign uses all the above possibilities in a purposeful instruction of the public; it ought therefore to be directed by journalists, who have, in addition to experience, the flair to recognise the publicity value of every news item. It follows that in EEC markets journalists who are familiar with member-countries should be responsible for public relations. The relevant organisation in Germany is the *Deutsche Public Relationsgesellschaft*, Flingernstrasse 68, Düsseldorf. The corresponding British organisation is the Institute of Public Relations, Hastings House, Norfolk Street, London, W.C.1. The American equivalent is the Public Relations Society of America, with Headquarters in Chicago.

D. SALES ORGANISATION

Firms already exporting enjoy the most immediate possibilities of enlarging sales within the EEC. They should examine the possibility of increasing their sales. The time is now favourable also for a new start by those firms which have not as yet exported. Investigations are needed to establish whether some products might sell better in other Common Market countries than in the home market; whether higher prices might be obtained; what action should be taken. Potential requirements and the state of competition must be investigated and all other previously mentioned factors need to be analysed.

Purchasing power, *i.e.* the level of income of the average household, is, in most cases, the major factor influencing demand. This applies particularly to the relatively highly priced consumer durables—cars, television-sets, radios, refrigerators and washing machines. Establishing a reliable service organisation for these products is extremely important. In all cases, as previously mentioned, the requirements of potential users must be examined before entering a new market.

In the home market, the effect of foreign competitors on the market position must be observed. The French food industry, for example, has achieved a remarkable success. A number of French provision firms (producers of speciality cooked foods, wine, cheese, cooking oils and drinks) have succeeded in extending their sales-outlets in other EEC countries from specialised high-grade grocery businesses to supermarkets and department stores. Clients and representatives should draw the attention of the home firm to such foreign competition.

I ADJUSTMENTS TO NEW CONDITIONS

The increasing integration of the Common Market raises the question as to whether it is desirable or necessary to make a change in the sales organisation.

The sales organisation which would correspond most nearly

to the character and requisites of a fully integrated Common Market would be one closely akin to that required for the home market. The advantage of such an organisation lies in its effective central control, in that some at least of the leading positions abroad can be filled by the personnel of the central organisation who can utilise their close connection with the central office in guiding their sections. On the other hand, it would not be altogether desirable to employ only nationals of the firm concerned. Experience shows that such a policy might encourage a latent fear, at least within a significant minority of the population in all European countries, of losing economic control to foreigners. This factor could adversely influence the firm's prospects. Local personnel, therefore, should be employed whenever possible, and this applies also to senior positions in the firm. Such personnel should be given several weeks' training at the Head Office.

The concept of independent foreign sales organisations conflicts in some respects with the idea of the Common Market as a single market. Nevertheless, independent sales organisations are likely to continue in many cases because changes in old and well-established relations would be impracticable. Sales through such well-established and deep-rooted organisations naturally enjoy numerous advantages. They do, however, adversely affect in many instances a homogeneous and rational production and sales policy.

The decision whether to centralise or de-centralise depends on many separate factors. The following rule, however, has general validity: when building up *new* sales organisations, the home sales organisation should form the basis; when independent sales organisations abroad are *already* well established, a common policy should be sought, particularly since the Common Market seeks to promote harmonisation. Integration with the central sales organisation should be attempted, using a step-by-step approach.

Sales within the Common Market should be based on progressive rationalisation. Technical rationalisation through the introduction of modern electrical office machines deserves mention, together with co-operative sales effort with other firms dealing in related or complementary products.

II ADJUSTMENTS IN WHOLESALE AND RETAIL TRADE

The wholesale and retail trade is frequently forgotten when discussing Common Market problems, but it deserves consideration. The response of the retail trade to the European market is shown in particular by the tendency to place greater stress on the country from which products originate. Special sales-promotion efforts on these lines have met with great success—for example, the sale of French or Italian products during well-planned "national" weeks. This sort of thing enables the retail trade to introduce an attractive new note in its shop windows, and at the same time to make high-quality foreign products available to purchasers whose appetite has been stimulated by foreign travel.

To date, too little regard has been paid to the increasing possibilities of mail order firms within the Common Market. These firms have the resources and are well placed to make available substantial capital for a first introduction of products in foreign markets.

E. BUYING

Principles similar to those regarding sales apply to the use of new sources of supply. New purchasing opportunities in other EEC countries are especially important to firms purchasing raw materials and semi-manufactured goods, for example, tanners, leather manufacturers and textile manufacturers. The growing difference between the declining internal Common Market tariffs and the external tariffs will particularly affect raw materials carrying high customs duties.

I FACTORS IN PURCHASING POLICY IN EEC

Investigation is needed to establish whether EEC countries in future might supply products more advantageously than other previous suppliers. Quality might possibly be better, or delivery dates might be shorter, or repeat orders might be easier, or reduction in inter-Common Market tariffs might favourably affect prices. In long-term contracts, account should be taken of price changes due to declining tariffs. The larger the market, the greater the possibility of purchasing cheaply. On the other hand, purchasing risks increase. Very careful investigation is therefore required of the possibilities both of increasing purchases from EEC countries and of switching purchases of products which so far have been obtained outside Europe. Here again market investigation is of great value. As already mentioned, it is not good policy to restrict market investigations to sales alone. Market investigations should also cover purchasing opportunities; indeed this has long been one of its most enduring and successful functions. When investigating potential supplies the following factors are important:

1. Existing purchasing possibilities in EEC countries.

2. Sales delivery and payment conditions in the individual countries.

3. The trend in purchasing opportunities having regard to commercial and political developments.

The possibility of co-operating with other firms should be considered when evaluating a possible switch to new suppliers. The costs of EEC products might be further reduced by establishing subsidiaries in the appropriate countries. In regard to co-operating with other firms in purchases, the French example of combining in a purchasing association is instructive. Finally, purchasing offices and purchasing agencies could profitably be established.

In some instances co-operating with a foreign purchasing association might be practicable, based possibly on purchases

for each other in the respective countries. In time the relation-
ship could become permanent.

In France, large trading chains established for purchasing
in the Common Market area are of increasing importance. To
date, their activity has been limited to foodstuffs but in future
they are likely to expand to cover all consumer goods and even
investment goods, at least in so far as these are mass-produced.

II RATIONAL STOCKHOLDING POLICY

A rational stockholding policy is of increasing importance.
Such a policy should include:

1. Adjusting the value of stocks to the larger turnover of a
   larger market.

2. The impact of different seasons in other EEC countries
   and of shifts in transport movements on the stockholding rhythm.

3. Regular control on different types of stock.

4. Restrictions on the tendency to larger stockholding and
   increased variety in stocks due to the larger market. (In
   individual cases, however, an increasing variety in stock
   may be required.)

A. FREIGHT AND CUSTOMS

In contrast to the provision of the Coal and Steel Community, the EEC Treaty has had no effect to date on the transportation policy of individual firms because a common transport policy has not yet been evolved. A common transport policy will, however, have important consequences. For example, the competitive position of the South German iron and steel industry has been considerably affected by the policy of the Coal and Steel Community. Previously, freights were calculated on the assumption of journey-end at the frontier; now calculations take no account of the frontier.

The effects of the EEC on customs tariffs are important. After the transition period, which will end at the latest on 31st December 1969, tariffs between EEC countries will disappear completely. On 1st January 1962, tariffs between EEC countries were reduced by 40 per cent for industrial products. This rapid reduction in internal tariffs has to be seen in relation to the gradual implementation of the common external tariff affecting trade with countries outside the Community. Details of tariffs are available in Britain from the Board of Trade, and in the United States from the Superintendent of Documents, Government Printing Office.

The progressive changes in tariffs are of importance both to a firm's purchases and to its sales. With regard to purchases: a growing number of firms are increasing their imports from EEC countries or at least are continuously watching the improving purchasing opportunities from such countries. Equally, with regard to export-sales, the reduction in inter-EEC tariffs facilitates the export of products to other EEC states. The following table lists German customs tariffs on 1st January 1962 and shows in particular the significant impact of tariffs on the competitive position of suppliers from EEC countries and from third countries.

Imports from

	Common Market Countries	Other Countries	Common External Tariffs
Cameras	3·5	8·6	18
Cars up to 2 litres	10·0	18·9	29
Cars above 2 litres	12·5	23·2	29
Butter	17·5	24·0	24
Beef	14·0	20·0	20
Sewing machines	3·5	7·1	12
Typewriters	7·0	12·8	16

I INTERNAL COMMON MARKET TARIFFS

(a) INDUSTRIAL PRODUCTS

On 1st January 1962, customs duties were reduced by a further 10 per cent of their value at 1st January 1957, *i.e.* of the so-called "originating tariffs". Consequently, on 1st January 1962, internal tariffs have been reduced by a total of 40 per cent from their original value. The Council of Ministers of the EEC has meanwhile decided on a further reduction of 10 per cent. From 1st July 1962, total reductions will amount to 50 per cent of the original value.

(b) AGRICULTURE

Customs tariffs on non-liberalised agricultural products were reduced on 1st January 1962 by a further 5 per cent, after an additional reduction of 5 per cent on 1st January 1961 due to the decision to speed up liberalisation of 12th May 1960. Tariffs on liberalised products were reduced by 10 per cent on 1st January 1962. All agricultural tariffs have therefore been reduced by

30 per cent from the original value at 1st January 1957. A further reduction applies from 1st March 1962 for non-liberalised agricultural products.

II EXTERNAL TARIFFS

(a) INDUSTRIAL PRODUCTS

Tariffs specifically reduced due to boom conditions (*i.e.* tariffs on all products except those on the "protected list") were again increased on 1st January 1961, due to the withdrawal of the first half of this concession. On 1st January 1962, the second half of the tariff concession was withdrawn.

The first movements to harmonise national tariffs to a common external tariff were inaugurated on 1st January 1961, although the original date had been 1st January 1962. Differences between the original tariffs on 1st January 1957 and the intended common tariffs were reduced by 30 per cent. The intended common tariff reduced by 20 per cent was used as a basis. In most products in Germany, harmonisation has increased tariffs to third countries.

On 1st January 1962 some tariff reductions which had been conceded by West Germany to Switzerland became inoperative, so that tariffs were increased on these products.

As soon as the Dillon discussions are completed, the ultimate EEC external tariffs are likely to be altered. These changes, however, will only influence existing national tariffs in exceptional cases since harmonisation has been based on a 20 per cent reduced common tariff and concessions to third countries are unlikely to exceed this limit.

(b) AGRICULTURE

In contrast to industrial tariffs, agricultural tariffs were not affected by the acceleration decision of 12th May 1960, and the first steps in harmonising external agricultural tariffs were taken on 1st January 1962.

Differences between the original tariffs on 1st January 1957 and the common external tariffs were reduced by 30 per cent.

Western Germany's tariffs were in some cases reduced since its agricultural products to some extent enjoyed higher tariff protection than the EEC external tariff.

All departments of a firm should have available for consideration data on the development of customs tariffs in European markets.

B. LOCATION POLICY IN THE EUROPEAN MARKET

The expansion of the economies of the Six so noticeable since the beginning of the Common Market has partly created new industrial centres and partly strengthened existing European industrial areas, *i.e.* industrial concentration in areas already particularly active in production. New industrial concentrations in EEC countries have developed recently in Northern Italy (around Turin and Milan), in Provence (centred on Lyons), and in south-east Netherlands (Arnhem–Nijmegen). Firms should pay heed to these developments particularly if decisions are required on the location of new factories, storage depots, assembly plants, service organisations and new sales networks.

It is essential to take cognisance of Common Market regional policies favouring certain localities. These areas, favoured by the regulations of the EEC Treaty, include, amongst others, the zonal border areas of the German Federal Republic, Southern Italy and Sicily. The European Investment Bank and the European Social Fund are likely to provide considerable financial assistance to these areas. In addition the EEC Commission has considered the possibility of establishing development nuclei in the border areas of the Common Market countries. It is acknowledged that suitable firms need to be attracted to ensure progress in underdeveloped areas within the Community. Consequently new industrial areas are to be created, or existing industrial nuclei will be extended in four or five peripheral zones, each at a cost of about £60–£80 million. In late 1961, the Common Market Commission authorised investigation of the following three projects:

1. Establishment of an industrial development nucleus in Southern Italy.

2. Water exchange between the Province of Luxemburg (Belgium) and Lorraine.

3. Development of tourist trade in Corsica and Sardinia.

Firms should also observe developments outside EEC countries. For example, in the Danish and Swedish border areas of the Common Market a new industrial concentration is developing around Gothenburg (Göteborg).

I FACTORS IN DETERMINING LOCALITY

The decision whether to establish a subsidiary or to manufacture part of output in another EEC country must be taken on the merits of each individual case. The decision should, however, be influenced by longer-term considerations of the growing unification of the economies of the six EEC countries, and also by the Common Market regional policies.

The following considerations apply in determining locality:

1. The developing sales opportunities in the Common Market.

2. The firm's intention with regard to its share of the market.

3. Planning of production and sales having regard to the above-mentioned considerations.

4. The labour market and other external considerations (for example, transportation).

II FACILITIES FROM PUBLIC AUTHORITIES

A firm may reasonably expect the relevant authorities to assist its efforts in creating new employment opportunities. National or local authorities can help by:

1. Making available industrial sites.
2. Construction and lease of factories.
3. Assistance in housing for employees.
4. Purchase of industrial sites.
5. Improvement in transportation facilities.
6. Suitable arrangements for training and recreation.

C. STANDARDS

I STANDARDISATION AND HARMONISATION

Complete liberalisation and harmonisation within the EEC may still fail to lead to complete economic integration if different standards in individual EEC countries create insurmountable difficulties for business. In office machinery, for example, foreign firms cannot compete in other EEC countries because their products are based on different standards.

Standards are a difficult and complex subject. The following example will prove the point. Basic changes in standards require prior notice of at least four months so that manufacturers and users may express their views. In June 1960, users —in the main engineering firms—were informed that standard 2448 (tubes) was to be changed in conformity with an international standard office recommendation based on international discussions. Steel tube manufacturers in Germany, as well as in other European countries, had altered their production to conform to these new standards of external pressure and wall thicknesses. A new standard form DIN 2448, which included technical explanations, was attached. The proposal involved a technical change in long-established construction methods which in practice could not easily be realised. Consequently users expressed considerable disquiet. Finally standard 2448 was redrafted, taking into account the wishes of users.

This example shows that users give serious consideration to new proposals affecting standards, and that they must take account of the fact that international interests may determine changes in standards.

The importance of standards in European business integration may increase sharply should Britain with its entirely different weights and measures join the Common Market. (Britain has recently changed to Centigrade temperatures. It is hoped that this is a good beginning to the harmonisation of British standards with those on the Continent.) Experts consider that harmonisation of standards is of such importance that a failure in this field could endanger economic integration. This applies also in situations not at all obvious at first sight. Competition can be substantially influenced by lack of similarity in packaging and product description, as in the case, for example, of margarine.

Finally it should be noted that German standards translated into English (over 1,100), into Spanish (over 700) and into French (approximately 200) can be obtained from Beuth-Vertrieb GmbH., Uhlandstr. 175, Berlin, W.15.

II INTERNATIONAL CO-OPERATION ON STANDARDS

A continuous effort to further international co-operation in standards is desirable in addition to what has been said so far. Industry should not simply react to proposals; in its own interests, and those of the economy at large, industry should take the initiative in stressing that successful international specialisation of trade and production requires maximum possible international harmonisation of standards.

The International Organisation for Standards (ISO), founded in Geneva in 1946, is the most important body amongst the organisations responsible for international standards. Its objects include:

1. Recommendations for co-ordination of standards by all participating countries. (At present 47 countries participate, including the countries of Eastern Europe.)

2. Formulation of international standards.

3. Initiative in formulating new standards.

4. Mutual exchange of information among users (*i.e.* members in the national organisations responsible for standards).

5. Co-operation with other international organisations.

At present, 104 technical committees and technical sections, having their own secretariats, are responsible for practical work. The National Standards Organisation of each country acts as secretariat to individual technical committees. The technical committees form sub-committees and working parties according to requirements.

In addition to this world-wide co-operation, a European standards organisation was founded in 1960 with the object of harmonising and facilitating economic integration. It is particularly encouraging that this organisation includes not only the EEC countries, but also those of the European Free Trade Area (EFTA). The committee is known as the *Comité Européen de Coordination des Normes* (CEN). It meets in Paris, the French Standards Committee providing the secretariat. The *Comité Européen* seeks to harmonise as far as necessary the standards of member countries.

The EEC Commission has also shown active interest in this field. Soon after the signing of the Treaty of Rome, it stated that differing standards and differing safety requirements considerably influence internal trade with the Community. According to the Commission, lack of co-ordination is especially noticeable in the manufacture of weighing machines—the lack of standard testing regulations creates great difficulties—and in the manufacture of motor vehicle components.

As a first step the Commission sent two questionnaires to member countries with the long-term object of harmonising standards of vehicle construction and the short-term object of harmonising regulations with regard to the dimensions of motor vehicle numbers, the size and power of car-lights, and the colour and angle-of-illumination of "blink" direction indicators. Unfortunately, not all member-states have yet completed the questionnaires. The following working parties dealing with standards indicate the subjects dealt with by the Commission:

Safety requirements
Pharmaceutical products
Paint
Components and replacement parts in vehicles
Tractors
Agriculture

D. COMPARISON OF COMPETING PRODUCTS

Comparing competing products illustrates the significance of industrial design. The importance of design does not require stressing at a time when the design of the Scandinavian home furnishing industry has achieved outstanding success. The entrepreneur needs to be personally aware of what is being done in various countries so as to be familiar with current trends in industrial design. As a matter of export policy, products in which design plays a crucial part should be directed to those countries where similar tastes predominate.

European trade would be much facilitated if a common industrial style should become current in all EEC countries. Design would then cease to be an obstacle to trade within the Community. This, however, lies in the future, although as a first step a committee has been set up in Brussels consisting of representatives of institutions responsible for promoting international design in the six Common Market countries. At its first meeting observers from the Community's administration supported the initiative and indicated the areas of possible co-operation between the Committee and the relevant authorities of EEC countries. Representatives of individual countries exchanged views on the situation and the possible use of industrial design.

This approach is equally applicable to the problem of taste in individual EEC countries. When comparing, for example, German taste with Sicilian, it is apparent that bright gay colours are preferred in Sicily, whereas in the northern areas of the Federal Republic the tendency is towards undemonstrative, quiet colours.

Taste is particularly important with regard to products of the food industry. Until taste conforms in Europe to a similar extent as in the United States, a firm must take note of trends of taste in the different EEC countries.

It may prove advantageous to set up test units within EEC countries to find out habits regarding choice of raw materials, technical suitability and finishing processes. These units, which would in practice be production laboratories, in co-operation with local labour, would find out how to satisfy the wishes of purchasers in these countries. A German shoe manufacturer did useful pioneering work in this field by establishing a subsidiary in Italy and has benefited greatly from the experience gained.

Point Six
Co-operating with other Firms

A. SALES CO-OPERATIVES AND MUTUAL SHAREHOLDING

Co-operation between firms is becoming more and more marked. A German firm which supplements, for example, the production programme of a French firm, attaches itself thereby to the French organisation to its own advantage, for then it does not need to establish a separate sales organisation in France.

Here again the French example is significant. In France, craft organisations in the machine-tool trade and wholesalers and retailers have formed co-operatives to strengthen their sales in Common Market countries. Equally mutual shareholdings between firms in EEC countries have become very important. Another aspect of Common Market policy affects inter-member shareholding. The Treaty of Rome looks forward to the liberalisation of movement of capital. The first liberalisation measures have been carried through, and the shares of other EEC countries are now listed in practically all stock exchanges within the Community.

Inter-firm comparisons are an important aspect of co-operation between firms. A firm requires knowledge of its position in relation to competitors. Knowledge of where it enjoys a comparative advantage and where it is lagging is particularly important.

Cost comparisons are also an important element in inter-firm comparisons. These provide important data determining the price policy of firms. Inter-firm comparisons are equally significant in trade enterprises because trading organisations as a rule are more alike than industrial firms. Therefore more significant data are frequently obtainable.

B. LICENSING

Licensing requires serious consideration by industry, particularly by German industry. In this field, Germany unfortunately shows a continuous negative balance which in the years 1958 to 1960 approximated to about 150 million DM for the EEC area.

In a discussion on "Licensing Abroad", the Working Committee of the Chamber of Industry and Trade in Baden-Württemberg indicated, amongst others, the following motives for licensing foreign firms:

1. Maintaining a foreign market, even when imports are restricted.

2. Maintaining exports at least in the form of additional requirements.

3. Covering third markets which cannot be supplied directly either due to foreign exchange difficulties or for price reasons.

Reassessment of licensing policy may prove advantageous in view of the opening up of the European market.

Point Seven

Adjusting the Firm's Character to Integration

A. INFORMATION SERVICE WITHIN THE FIRM

It is not enough for leading executives alone to give consideration to the problems of the Common Market. Admittedly, when the EEC was first established its problems were in the main relevant only to top executives. Today, however, after the completion of the first stage of the transition period, the movement towards integration is sufficiently powerful to affect practically all departments of a firm. Information material on Common Market matters should therefore be transmitted to all departments so as to reach all concerned. The information contained in the *Official Journal of the European Community* is particularly important. The relevant newspapers and periodicals should be made available, and also the publications of the numerous high-quality information services.

European topics should be dealt with in house journals so as to familiarise employees with the purposes and imperatives of the Common Market. This would have the additional advantage that other Common Market countries would no longer be considered as remote places "at the back of beyond". In consequence, the transfer of personnel to subsidiaries in other EEC countries would be psychologically facilitated. In addition, house magazines should discuss local employees' approach and attitude to their foreign colleagues.

B. DEPARTMENTAL REORGANISATION

Various methods may be used for instructing individual departments of the firm in the problems of European integration and particularly in the increasing activities of the EEC authorities. Organisation within the firm is an important factor, but by no means the only important factor. The personnel involved is decisive. Within the firm, those concerned with Common Market economic matters require proper knowledge of languages and personnel connections with the relevant organisations. These "Europeans" in the firm must have the necessary influence in relation to other interests and personalities. Information must be followed by action. The objective should be for the whole firm to be well informed on integration, so that it can as a body direct its efforts towards, and be active in promoting, the closer integration of the Community.

In the case of medium- and small-sized firms, the solution is simple. In such cases, the all-round man—preferably the manager of the foreign trade and advertising section—is normally entrusted with Common Market questions. Frequently the managing director's assistant is expected to look after European interests in addition to his other jobs.

Some large firms have established a separate section at head office to deal with European integration questions. This may be a good solution provided that the department co-operates closely and harmoniously with other sections and takes the initiative in stimulating activity. Above all, it is important to eliminate the impression that the Common Market is solely relevant to the section dealing with foreign trade. Integration affects all departments of the firm: the European market is steadily becoming the home market. For this reason, it is worth considering the action of some firms which have combined sales to Europe with the section for home sales, regarding as "foreign trade" only their sales to non-European countries.

Integration in the long run may require complete reorganisation in many firms. For example, one large firm, which before the Common Market was established had obtained most of its products from the home market, has now doubled its staff in the Import and Customs Department dealing with imports from abroad.

However much the internal structure of firms may differ, the following departments in the majority of them will probably need enlarging:

    Market research
    Advertising
    Sales and Buying (Europe)
    Translation (French, English, Italian)

Point Eight
Examining the Firm's Program Planning

A. STANDARDS

Standards have been dealt with separately in view of their importance (see Point Five, C: pp. 55–8).

B. SPECIALISATION

The Common Market's tendency is to encourage specialisation. The main purpose of a large market is to induce firms to specialise. Specialisation may take various forms:

(i) of the product;
(ii) of production methods;
(iii) of raw materials and equipment used.

Specialisation in sales outlets is also possible. One may decide, for example, to reduce the number of the existing types of outlets and concentrate on one or the other.

I ADVANTAGES OF SPECIALISATION

High production is possible in a limited sector. Consequently a market sector can be established in which competition is not too severe and a certain freedom in pricing policy is possible. In certain circumstances a position approaching a monopoly might be created.

II DISADVANTAGES OF SPECIALISATION

Fluctuations in demand may become pronounced; but adequate market research should foresee changes in market conditions. Undoubtedly in some cases a broadening of production and sales program may be desirable, but most firms appear to suffer from maintaining too wide a range of products.

III SOME GERMAN EXAMPLES OF SPECIALISATION

Several examples of co-operation between German firms and other firms in EEC countries are mentioned below:

Machine tool factories: exchange of technical information on new products.

Barrel manufacture: suspension of production of barrel types in small demand, concentration on standard types through a rationalisation programme.

Oil hydraulics: technical co-operation, a standardised construction of oil hydraulic plant.

The following example is instructive in showing a medium-sized firm's successful approach. A factory in Hessen producing cash- and deed-boxes had to plan its adaptation to the new market conditions of the EEC. The manager decided that, in order to establish an overall picture, he required a personal impression of the situation in the various EEC countries. He visited them and in each purchased the products of competitors. Finally he carefully considered the various competing products and developed a product-type which he believed he would be able to sell everywhere within the EEC area. Calculating on a substantial increase in turnover, he was able to offer the new product cheaply and succeeded in penetrating the markets in the various countries.

C. LIMITATION OF TYPES

Careful consideration should also be given to limiting the range of products. Concentration on those types having largest sales potential is essential in a large market. An investigation of the costs of the various types and potential returns is essential.

Point Nine
Utilising Credit Possibilities

Capital required for essential investments by firms in order to meet Common Market conditions may be obtained from European credit sources. The European Investment Bank makes funds available for financing specific projects. The European Social Fund, however, provides only indirect support. These two organisations will be discussed at a later stage. (See pp. 140-2.) In Appendices IV and V other credit possibilities available in Western Germany are listed.

DEVELOPMENT FUND TENDERS

German firms to date have not taken a significant part in tendering for contracts offered by the EEC Development Fund. Large sectors of German industry still appear to be unaware of these contracts.

The reason for this lack of initiative by German firms is not clear. It may be due to the traditional connections, frequently strengthened by personal relationships, between the former colonial powers in the Community (*i.e.* France and Holland) and the newly independent states in Africa and Asia. All the same, new business should be sought in these countries and regular visits by agents should be arranged.

In Britain, the *Official Journal of the European Community* is the relevant source of information in this field. The *Board of Trade Journal* also publishes information on contracts open for tender. In the United States, information of this kind is available from the European Community Information Service, Suite 88, the Farragut Building, Washington 6, D.C.

Point Ten

Dealing with Problems of the Labour Market

Lack of labour is acknowledged as one of the most difficult problems of business policy. All possible means of attracting qualified workers require investigation. A firm should look now to the EEC area as its labour source in view of the complete liberalisation of the labour market within the Community by the end of the transition period. Two approaches are possible:

A. STUDYING FOREIGN LABOUR MARKETS

Regular surveys are needed to locate labour and labour reserves in individual Common Market countries. In several areas in these countries labour reserves are still available. Southern Italy and the Italian islands should be considered. Greece, which is now associated with the Common Market, should not be forgotten.

B. WELFARE OF FOREIGN WORKERS

The interests of foreign workers should be carefully considered so as to encourage their full participation within the firm. Some hints are given below:

1. The foreign worker should be instructed on his rights and duties. (Wage notification should be in his own language as well as that of the "host country".)

2. He should have access to managers assisted by interpreters.

3. Suitable accommodation, including working facilities, should be provided.

4. Language courses should be arranged.

5. Recreational opportunities should be provided.

Broadcasting stations have recently started to help in welfare efforts. Both the Bavarian radio station and the West German Broadcasting Corporation are now transmitting programs for Italian workers in the Federal Republic. Firms should draw the attention of workers to these programs. Some businesses have actually taken part in them. This is a praiseworthy example.

Employment of foreign labour with its specific problems has ceased to be the concern of only a few firms. At the end of 1961, more than 550,000 foreigners were employed in Western Germany, of whom 225,000 were Italians, 62,000 Spaniards and 53,000 Greeks. The Federal Association of German Employers (*Bundesvereinigung der Deutschen Arbeitgeberverbände*, Hansaring 42, Cologne) has published a series of "Regulations to be observed in recruitment and employment of foreign workers".

Point Eleven
Basic Vocational and Further Training

A. COMMUNITY POLICY ON VOCATIONAL TRAINING

The objects of the Common Market Treaty include improving employment opportunities for labour within the Community and furthering liberalisation of local and trade restrictions on employment. *Article 128* of the Common Market Treaty states that, acting on the proposal of the Commission and after consultation with the Economic and Social Committee, the Council of Ministers should establish general principles for a common policy on vocational training in order to facilitate harmonious economic progress of the individual economies as well as of the Common Market as a whole.

On the basis of this decision, the Common Market Commission in 1961 worked out "Basic Principles of a common policy for vocational training in the Common Market countries". These will probably be accepted early in 1963. The member-states will then publish the appropriate regulations. In the countries of the Community, the Chambers of Industry and Commerce are the principle supporters of craft and trade training. In this field further tasks require their attention.

These "Basic Principles" (ten in number) evolved by the Common Market Commission aim at harmonising qualifications in member countries while leaving individual countries a free choice in the methods of training to be adopted. These principles may be summarised as follows:

The various systems of apprentice and trade training in individual countries are to be further developed, but not basically altered. It is held that member states should be completely free to decide whether apprentice and trade education should be furthered in schools or within firms.

The Common Market Commission seeks to ensure that the

product and the level of education in the Community should
be comparable, so that trained personnel of one country can
take up employment in other countries. The Commission's
program also seeks to ensure that everyone receives an
adequate and appropriate education. Disadvantageous interruptions between general school education and the start of
vocational training should be avoided, and close connection
should be established between schooling and vocational
training, so that training may be better adapted to the requirements of industry.

A comparable educational level is to be obtained by harmonising the different examinations and by interchanging experience
within the member states. It is proposed also to evaluate examinations on a similar basis and to establish European
competitions.

Vocational training assists also in increasing the labour supply
in line with the increasing demand for skilled labour. For
example, special training programs to promote the training of
Italian workers have been considered. A special approach to
training is justified also in occupations facing specific structural
problems—for example, agriculture, transport and handicrafts.

The financing of training programs is not considered to
be the task of the Community. Community financing would
be justified only for special programs and special institutions
within the Common Market, such as model establishments for
craft training, European Apprentice Training Institutions, new
Teachers' Training Colleges, and the transformation of national
educational institutions into European institutions.

It has been suggested that an advisory committee should be
established for vocational training to assist the Common
Market Commission in meeting its tasks in this field as outlined in *Article 128* of the Common Market Treaty. One-third
of the members of this committee would consist of representatives of governments, one-third of employees, and one-third of
employers.

B. FURTHER EDUCATION

The European Economic Community has rightly been called "the greatest experiment in economic history". Its success depends substantially on whether the present and future managerial group in Europe (estimated by an American authority to number about 175,000) can meet the problems generated by the Common Market. The present entrepreneur or manager will maintain his position only if he is fully acquainted with the structure of the Common Market. For this reason training and further education in the problems of the European market is essential for managing directors as well as for apprentices.

I GERMAN EXAMPLES

Numerous personalities and organisations have acknowledged the necessity of intensive training for the European market, but in practice this has been neglected by a number of firms. On the European level, discussions are continuing about the European University in Florence proposed in the Euratom Treaty. This university will open probably this year. Several German universities—for example, Hamburg, Cologne and Saarbrücken—have excellent institutions within the framework of the Faculties of Economics and Social Science and the Legal Departments. Nearly all the German institutions for training and further education mentioned in the publication *Development of Leadership*—published by *Deutsches Institut zür Förderung des industriellen Führungsnachwuchses* (German Institute for the Development of Future Industrial Leaders), Mehlemer Str. 18, Cologne—include European subjects in their teaching curricula.

The *C. Rudolf Poensgen Institute* for furthering the training of future leaders in industry (founded in Düsseldorf in June 1956 by the local Chamber of Industry and Trade) deserves mention by way of example. This Foundation serves to train younger leaders in industry, to communicate results and experience in the subject of leadership technique, and to support research. The training courses for future leaders are designed to meet these objectives. Those taking part will be prepared for the growing requirements likely to occur during the coming years. Special account is taken of changes in markets, in production, in sales, in finance, as well as of the techniques of management (planning, development, business policy and administration). Naturally, in view of these aims, the subject of the European market plays an important part not only in the basic curriculum, but also in special courses and conferences. For example, in 1960 the Institute arranged a course on "The Firm's Business Policy and Conflicting Factors in European Integration", while in the late autumn of 1961 it organised a special meeting in Brussels dealing with international economic problems of the Common Market Commission. Members of the Commission discussed working arrangements and objectives in the following subjects: competition, social policy, trade cycle policy, regional policy, as well as trade and currency policy. Appendix VII describes in more detail activities in Western Germany in this field.

The Federal Republic has no institution comparable with the French *Institut Européen d'Administration des Affaires* (INSEAD) in Fontainebleau, which trains European-orientated business administrators. The interest of the German business man in European training and further education is still underdeveloped, if not completely undeveloped. The first essential is to appreciate that today all entrepreneurs and business men, irrespective of their position within the hierarchy, require a Common Market orientation. For this reason, arrangements outside firms are in many cases insufficient, quite apart from the fact that frequently they fail to attract adequate interest. For example, the arrangements of a well-established educational institution towards the end of 1961 had to be abandoned because of lack of interest.

II RECOMMENDATIONS FOR ACTION BY FIRMS

What are the possibilities open to individual firms? Here are some proposals for action:

(a) INSTRUCTION ON THE EUROPEAN MARKET WITHIN THE FIRM

1. Encouraging all suitable employees to read appropriate journals and relevant literature.

2. Regular discussions (about every two months) on detailed problems of the European market.

3. Regular conferences at headquarters of agents in EEC countries.

4. Regular lectures, preferably with visual aids, attended by as many employees as possible.

(b) ENCOURAGING EMPLOYEES TO TAKE PART IN

1. the activities of training and further educational instruction

2. visits to other European countries

3. exchange of personnel.

The business man should seek to ensure, within the framework of what is practicable, that business training in commercial and business colleges, as well as universities, should be directed more intensively to the European Common Market. The founding of the Begemann commercial school (Kaiserstrasse 33, Frankfort-on-Main)—which trains its pupils in London during the first year, in Geneva during their second, and in Frankfort in their third year—shows a growing appreciation of the fact that the best chances of success are available only to those who combine an excellent knowledge of languages with a good knowledge of the economic aspects of the EEC. Trainee-exchanges are arranged by *Carl Duisberg-Gesellschaft*, Kaiser-Friedrich-Ufer 41–45, Cologne.

C. EUROPEAN BUSINESS TRAINING CENTRES

Relevant teaching and research institutes are listed below:

Teaching and research institutes

Bologna Centre of the School of Advanced International Studies at Johns Hopkins University — Bologna (*Italy*) 3, Largo Alfredo Trombetti *tel.* 2 37 77–2 38 57

Europa-College — Bruges (*Belgium*) 11, Dyver *tel.* 3 65 62

Institut Européen d'Administration des Affaires — Fontainebleau (*France*) Palais de Fontainebleau (S.-et-M.) *tel.* 931.25.39

Institut für das Recht der Europäischen Gemeinschaften in the University of Cologne — Lindenthal-Cologne (*West Germany*) Albertus-Magnus-Platz *tel.* 2 02 41

Centre Européen Universitaire — Nancy (*France*) 3, Place Stanislas *tel.* 52 77 50

Collège Européen des Sciences sociales et économiques — Paris VI (*France*) 183, boulevard Saint Germain *tel.* BABylone 08 55

Istituto di Studi Europei—Alcide de Gasperi	Rome (*Italy*) Viale Pola 12 *tel.* 846 806
Europäisches Forschungsinstitut of the University of the Saarland	Saarbrücken (*W. Germany*) Universität des Saarlandes *tel.* 2 16 51
Centre Universitaire des Hautes Etudes Européennes of the University of Strasbourg	Strasbourg (*France*) Place de l'Université
Institut Universitaire d'Etudes Européennes	Turin (*Italy*) Via Conte Rosso 3 *tel.* 55 32 69
Österreichisches College und Forschungsinstitut für Europäische Gegenwartskunde	Vienna IV (*Austria*) Argentinierstr. 21/1 *tel.* U 4 15 27
Instituto de Estudios Europeos	Barcelona (*Spain*) Via Layetana 32 *tel.* 22 000
Forschungsinstitut der Deutschen Gesellschaft für Auswärtige Politik	Bonn (*W. Germany*) Schaumburg-Lippe-Str. 6
Centre Européen de la Culture	Geneva (*Switzerland*) 122, rue de Lausanne *tel.* 32 66 15
Gesellschaft für Übernationale Zusammenarbeite. V.	Cologne (*W. Germany*) Hohenstaufenring 11 *tel.* 21 36 61
Centre de Recherches Européennes of the University of Lausanne	Lausanne (*Switzerland*) Hôtel de Ville *tel.* 21 53 78

Centre de Recherches et d'Etudes de Psychologie des Peuples et de Sociologie Economique	Le Havre (*France*) Boîte postale 258 *tel.* 42 47 55
"Europa-Institut" of the University of Leyden	Leyden (*Netherlands*) Rijksuniversiteit té Leiden Juridisch Studiecentrum "Gravensteen" Pieterkerkhof 6 *tel.* 0 17 10 : 2 13 48
Institut für Europäische Geschichte	Mainz (*W. Germany*) Alte Universitätsstr. 17 *tel.* 48 70
Institut für Kontinental-Europäische Forschung	Munich (*W. Germany*) Flughafen Riem *tel.* 47 00 48
Osteuropa-Institut	Munich (*W. Germany*) Scheinerstr. 11 *tel.* 48 38 21

This list includes only some of the many relevant institutes which to some extent co-operate closely together.

Point Twelve

Co-operation between Chambers of Commerce and Industrial Associations

The increase in European economic integration and the expected extension of the Common Market to other countries are creating difficult business problems. These difficulties are increased by the necessity of dealing with problems across national or language frontiers. Consequently firms have been encouraged to seek assistance from organisations which are well established internationally and which represent the interests of the economy as a whole or of specific sectors.

The increasing need of dealing with common European problems has encouraged large numbers of industrial institutions and organisations to establish associations with similar organisations in the six member states. What tasks relevant to individual firms are being undertaken by these associations? These can be divided into three groups.

(a) Collection of information.

(b) Passing information to members.

(c) Representing their respective business interests in dealings with the authorities of the European communities.

The collection of information depends above all on assembling objective statistical data on the EEC countries. These community-wide associations have also the task of informing members about technical and commercial developments. For this purpose basic data on the EEC must be assembled to be made available to members. In addition to collecting this data, the difficulties which still obstruct business within the EEC must be identified. These difficulties exist in spite of the elimination of many obstacles through specific action of the administration. The care of standards, previously cited (pp. 55–58), is a relevant example of the effectiveness of trade protests. Another example of successful action has been the protest of the respective industries against the unjustified limitation of car imports into Italy through manipulation of licences. This trading obstacle has been eliminated since 1st January 1962. The third activity of such European industrial associations covers representation to the authorities of the European Community. The provision of expert advice to the Commission is particularly important. The activities of these associations can be best described with reference to the example of the Standing Conference of the Chambers of Industry and Trade of the European Economic Community.

A. THE STANDING CONFERENCE OF THE CHAMBERS OF INDUSTRY AND TRADE OF THE EEC COUNTRIES

The organisation of the Standing Conference provides for two plenary sessions each year, one of which takes place in Brussels and the other in another EEC country. The activity of the Standing Conference, like that of individual Chambers of Industry and Commerce, is to reconcile and balance overall economic points of view.

Its members are:

1. Deutscher Industrie-und Handelstag, Bonn.

2. Assemblée des Présidents des Chambres de Commerce et d'Industrie de la Communauté, Paris.

3. Chambre de Commerce de Luxembourg.

4. Fédération Nationale des Chambres de Commerce et d'Industrie de Belgique, Brussels.

5. Kamer van Koophandel en Fabrieken voor Rotterdam, Rotterdam, and all other Dutch Chambers of Industry and Commerce.

    6. Unione Italiana delle Camere di Commercio, Industria e Agricoltura, Rome.

The President of the Standing Conference is elected for one year. His tasks include the chairmanship of plenary sessions and assuring continuity of work between individual plenary meetings. The present President is Dr. K. P. van der Mandele, Rotterdam.

I THE WORK OF THE CONFERENCE'S COMMITTEES

Committees are mainly responsible for the work of the Standing Conference. For example, there are: a legal and a taxation committee; committees for trade policy, sales, Associated Members, as well as for craft and trade training. (The last mentioned is a function of all national Chambers.) These committees are guided by certain individual delegations, which act as *Rapporteurs*, carrying out investigations in co-operation with other delegations and putting forward proposals. These proposals are exhaustively discussed in the plenary sessions and, after agreement, are passed on to the governments of the member states and to the Common Market Commission with a request for consideration. The Commission has frequently stated that it attaches particular value to the work of the Committees because it combines practical business experience with taking account of overall economic considerations.

RESULTS TO DATE

The Standing Conference has already dealt with large numbers of individual problems. For example, resolutions have been passed on free access to supply markets, relations with associated countries, as well as freedom of capital movements. All delegations have spoken in favour of a liberal purchasing policy by the economies of the EEC countries and of free access to world markets. Consequently they have expressed the view that the Common Market should not form a closed economic bloc, but should be an integrated member of a liberal world economy. A further resolution refers to the development of transport networks in the community.

II TRANSACTIONS WITH THE CHAMBERS OF EFTA COUNTRIES

The German delegation to the Standing Conference in particular has strongly pressed the view that European integration limited solely to the EEC might endanger free world trade. The Standing Conference has therefore encouraged relations with other countries and especially with the countries of EFTA.

At the request of the German delegation, the Standing Conference passed a resolution welcoming the greatest possible multilateral association with EFTA. The Standing Conference also resolved that national delegations should discuss with the Chambers of Industry and Commerce in EFTA countries proposals to be submitted to the respective governments, designed to obviate the dangers to the flow of trade due to the creation of two separate economic areas in Europe.

The German National Council of Industry and Commerce carried out discussions in 1959 and 1960 with representatives of the Swedish Chambers. It was found possible to reach agreement on the trade policy to be pursued in relation to overseas countries.

In addition to these German-Swedish meetings, there have been Dutch-Danish, Dutch-English, French-English, French-Swiss and Italian-Austrian discussions.

Apart from their immediate practical results, such bilateral discussions have great psychological value since they contribute to reducing or eliminating the tendency for attitudes to harden into those of a "bloc mentality".

The working atmosphere of the Standing Conference has continued to be harmonious, even friendly. In spite of different points of view on a number of individual problems, everyone has sought to find a formula acceptable to all members. In every case success has been achieved.

B. RELEVANT ORGANISATIONS

A firm may want to know the appropriate institution or organisation for obtaining information on specific market problems, business conditions, or organisations in the EEC countries.

If the problem of the firm concerns general economic or foreign trade policy, or tariff problems, the relevant Chamber of Industry or Commerce is the best source of information. This Chamber usually co-operates through representatives with other Chambers of EEC countries and the official organisations of the European Community. The national chambers of foreign trade which operate in all EEC countries can also be of assistance.

If the problem is a specifically industrial one, it is more advantageous to approach the relevant industrial organisations. Appendix IX lists the principal European industrial and trading organisations.

Consultants deserve special mention since they are frequently able to provide valuable advice due to their specific knowledge, experience and work.

Craft Trades in the EEC

It is sometimes falsely assumed that craft trades are unlikely to be affected by the Common Market. The increasing supply of products and, above all, increasing competition between the economies will affect craft trades even if they are not themselves exporters to other EEC countries. This applies *a fortiori* to that sector of the craft industry which competes with other trades or industries in Europe. In consequence the leading association of the German craft trades, the Central Association of German Crafts, and the German Chamber of Craft Trades have been particularly active in considering the problems of European integration. They have foreseen that the best scope for adjustment to the Common Market lies in encouraging further training, further education and above all in advising on exports of craft products. The central organisation at the *Deutschen Handwerks-Institut*, Munich, and five regional offices provide advice on craft trade exports. They deal with enquiries from foreign countries, advise on brochures and other sales literature, handle participation by their members in trade fairs, and render assistance in commercial dealings with firms abroad. The craft trade organisations intend in the near future to consider measures facilitating imports. Market research and the techniques of marketing craft products are to be encouraged.

PART II

EXPERIENCE TO DATE

**Preliminary survey of the effects of the European
Market on business initiative**

PRELIMINARY SURVEY OF THE EFFECTS OF THE EUROPEAN MARKET ON BUSINESS INITIATIVE

I Survey of the Federal Republic

A. FIRST REPORT OF THE DEUTSCHE INDUSTRIE-UND HANDELSTAG

Almost every day newspapers, periodicals and information services in the Federal Republic report specific activities of German firms in the Common Market. During 1961 the *Deutsche Industrie-und Handelstag* (German National Council of Industry and Commerce), the representative organisation of the Chambers of Commerce and Industry in the Federal Republic (including West Berlin), drew up a first "balance sheet" of the measures taken by German firms in adjusting to the Common Market and to EFTA. Its data are derived from questionnaires or personal visits to industrialists. The investigation aimed not only at establishing the measures taken to date, but also at stimulating interchanges of experience and views among German firms, and at ascertaining the practical difficulties which still hinder the realisation of the Common Market. These surveys were widely reported by the German press. German industry, making a better showing than some of its critics would have thought possible, actively participated in this open discussion of general economic problems. The German initiative has been copied in Belgium. The important *Chambre de Commerce de Bruxelles* has carried out a similar investigation. The results of the questionnaire of the *Deutsche Industrie-und Handelstag* may be summarised as follows:

1. Measures of adjustment are noted in nearly all branches of industry including commercial firms.

2. Not only large firms but also medium and small firms show measures of adjustment. Of firms reporting

specific action, 60 per cent were large, 30 per cent medium and 10 per cent small organisations.

3. The interest of German firms in problems of integration is larger than generally assumed. Nevertheless it is substantially less than that found in France, where there is a particularly vigorous interest in Common Market matters.

4. A thorough knowledge of foreign languages and particularly of French is of decisive importance in business activity in EEC countries. As a rule good knowledge of foreign languages is scarce.

5. Firms which to date have neither exported to nor imported from the Common Market areas show regrettably little or no interest in EEC problems. This attitude is based on a misunderstanding. The Common Market is not only a source of imports or a market for exports, but is a new economic area representing important new opportunities for sales, purchasing, capital and labour —opportunities which are of vital concern to all firms. In the not too distant future it will be the home market.

In more detail the following picture emerges:

I. CHANGE IN SALES AND BUYING ORGANISATION

In general, German firms concentrating on sales outside Europe have not changed their purchasing or sales organisation. The following industrial sectors reported only limited adjustments to date: constructional equipment, machine tools, agricultural machinery, mineral oil production and shipyards.

Firms in the following sectors have undertaken adjustments: coupling and brake-linings, meat and canned meat products, photographic equipment, timber, dressmaking, machine construction, paper, school furniture, sweets and confectionery, synchronous induction motors and the live-stock industry.

These measures of adjustment include establishing subsidiaries near the western borders of the Federal Republic, in response to the increasing tendency of Germany's EEC partners to establish new sales organisations in the immediate vicinity of the frontier. Sales organisations for coupling and brake-linings were established in Belgium and Holland. Importers established contact with Italian and French suppliers for agricultural machinery. Agencies in Common Market countries and EFTA (reported from Holland and Denmark) were established for synchronous induction motors and photographic equipment. In general, agencies in Common Market countries have been enlarged.

2. MARKET RESEARCH IN COMMON MARKET AND EFTA COUNTRIES

The following German industries are particularly active in market research in EEC and EFTA countries: chemicals, iron foundrying, food, blast-furnace manufacturing, machinery manufacturing, steel and rolling mills. The wholesale trade in semi-finished and consumer products, as well as in non-ferrous metals and a grocery chain, have also carried out similar investigations. Even retail traders in textiles are reported to be showing activity. Subsidiaries, Chambers of Commerce and Industry and Business Associates are frequently used for market observation. The steel industry has encouraged customer goodwill by means of visits by engineers and business men. The results so far of these efforts in market observations show the beginning of a kind of "bloc outlook". In some cases, admittedly in few only, there was a conflict between the most advantageous price and the desire to trade within one's own trading area.

3. ADVERTISING AND PUBLIC RELATIONS IN THE EEC AND EFTA

In general, activities in advertising, as well as in public relations, have increased in the Common Market and in EFTA countries.

The following sectors show increased activity: chemical

industry, iron foundries, the plastics-using industry, machine construction, steel and rolling mills.

It is noticeable that direct contact with customers is preferred to the use of agents. Printed matter and brochures in particular are used in seeking to establish contact and in public relations. For this purpose existing agencies in the Common Market countries are employed.

In contrast to the efforts of firms in other EEC countries, the Common Market is not exploited by German firms as an advertising slogan: the potential client is not addressed as "Common Market friend".

4. SUBSIDIARIES IN COMMON MARKET AND EFTA COUNTRIES

In Germany, the chemical and pharmaceutical industries, machinery manufacturers, medical instrument manufacturers and steel-casting industries report the establishment of subsidiaries. It is also interesting to note that retail traders have established subsidiaries in Common Market countries.

5. ASSEMBLY INDUSTRIES IN EEC AND EFTA COUNTRIES

German machinery manufacturers, including producers of agricultural machinery, have taken part in assembly work in Common Market and EFTA countries. The chemical industry, machinery construction industry and steel manufacturing firms have granted licences.

6. TRAINEE EXCHANGE IN EEC AND EFTA COUNTRIES

Exchange of trainees between firms in Common Market countries has grown appreciably. For some time now it has exceeded the corresponding exchange with all other non-EEC countries. Breweries, iron foundries, steel works, machine construction, together with the wholesale trade, are particularly active.

7. PARTICIPATION IN TRADE FAIRS IN EEC AND EFTA COUNTRIES

German participation in trade fairs and exhibitions in EEC and EFTA countries is substantially greater than in countries outside these areas. The same interest is shown in trade fairs in EFTA as in EEC countries. Practically all firms which exhibit at all are active in these areas.

8. PARTICIPATION IN EEC TENDERS

Most German firms show no active interest in EEC tenders. The food industry, iron foundries, steel works and the machine-tool industry have been the only participants. All firms stressed that the use of agencies is particularly useful.

9. ADJUSTMENTS IN PRODUCTION, RATIONALISATION AND STANDARDISATION

The German steel industry above all has been active in adjusting production, in rationalisation and in standardisation. One steel works has adapted its production to standards worked out by its EEC partners. Iron and steel foundries, the precision engineering and optical industries, as well as steel manufacturers, have taken action in rationalising and standardising their product to meet Common Market requirements.

10. INTEREST IN COMMON MARKET AND EFTA PROBLEMS

In the main, it is large firms which are interested in the development of the Common Market. They evaluate and use relevant literature and send their employees to attend public lectures. They also take part in seminars. Such arrangements, however, are unfortunately less frequent in the Federal Republic than in other important Common Market countries. In general the importance of information has not yet been fully recognised. In particular Common Market seminars for business men and managers are much less frequent in Western Germany than in France.

B. THE FIRST "BALANCE SHEET" FOR A FEDERAL STATE: BADEN-WÜRTTEMBERG

The Working Committee of the Chamber of Industry and Commerce in Baden-Württemberg has published the first complete analysis of overall economic effects in one Federal state. These results are summarised as follows:

I BASIC CONSIDERATIONS

Positive opportunities for firms due to the formation of the Common Market have been utilised as far as possible. However, in contrast to the steps taken by firms in other EEC countries, above all in France, actions taken by German firms have been determined more by boom conditions than by the influence of European integration. Many of the measures taken have applied equally to EFTA and to EEC countries. Most of them to date have concerned purchases and sales. German manufacturers increasingly are purchasing semi-manufactures from abroad for use in their factories. The main sources of these products are other EEC countries. This division of labour extends, however, also to countries outside the Community. In regard to sales, activity has consisted in strengthening market research, in advertising and in changes in sales organisation (for example, by establishing new sales outlets or rearranging sales areas). Reduction in product-range, adjustments in production, and agreements with firms in other EEC countries have been much less frequent. Where subsidiaries have been established in EFTA countries this has been the result of basic policy decisions rather than of the desire to obviate tariff discrimination.

Competition in the German market by Common Market partners has grown substantially, but so has competition from third countries. The different tax treatment of products crossing national frontiers has been a more important factor in encouraging competition by other Common Market countries than the actual reduction in tariffs.

Certain sectors of the wholesale and retail trade have responded to the Common Market to a substantially greater extent than industry. Textile wholesalers and retailers in substantial numbers have formed joint purchasing and sales associations, which, in addition to co-operative purchasing, undertake co-operative advertising and arrange exchange of younger personnel. This kind of co-operation extends also to EFTA as well as to EEC countries and to some extent even to third countries.

II EFFECT OF INTEGRATION AND ADJUSTMENT MEASURES IN INDIVIDUAL INDUSTRIES

I. MACHINERY AND THE MACHINE-TOOLS INDUSTRY

Competition in the Common Market area including Germany has increased. French, Italian and Dutch firms have come into the market and also subsidiaries of American and British firms. Competition is more in price and delivery dates than in quality. In machine tools, price differences of 10–30 per cent have been mentioned. The reasons for these price differences are believed to lie partly in increasing costs within the Federal Republic and partly in differences in taxation of export products. The latter applies particularly to French products. It is feared that German exports will be unable to offset increasing wage and material costs.

Offers by Dutch firms on the German market and by Italian firms on the French and German markets of bakery equipment are particularly noticeable. Foreign firms offer the advantage of lower prices and extended credits. The textile machinery industry reports similarly, and also states that French competition has increased substantially due to generous public support for research.

On the other hand, re-equipment and modernisation in EEC countries have stimulated increasing demand for German equipment, particularly for looms and knitting machinery.

The market position of firms in EFTA countries continues to be strong in special products. Increasing sales promotion by EFTA competitors is, however, noticeable. The German bakery equipment industry in particular reports difficulties due to tariff discrimination in favour of Britain.

Adjustment measures by firms to meet increased competition in EFTA countries include: extension of servicing facilities, strengthening of market observation, modernisation of products and consideration of specific requests by purchasers. Such requests include, for example, supply of production plans and output calculations which greatly facilitate subsequent production by purchasers.

Customs preference has partly reduced British competition in Belgium and Holland. Comparable advantages were not obtained in Italy because an increase in general taxation on imports offset the reduction in tariffs. In general, boom conditions to date have obviated disadvantageous effects. It is believed, however, that competition will increase, more especially in credits than in price. EEC competitors are reported to be prepared to offer credits of up to eight years even in the case of relatively small products. The necessity of adjusting production is acknowledged. In cases where subsidiaries for assembly or finishing have been established, these have been set up both in Common Market and EFTA countries. The machine-construction and machine-tool industries to date have taken little part in competing for tenders in the Common Market area.

2. METAL-WORKING INDUSTRY

Special products in this field have maintained their strong position even in EFTA countries. Price competition, where existing, has increased, particularly in the Dutch, Italian and German markets. The main competitors are subsidiaries of American and British firms in the EEC who enjoy the advantage of assembly line production and a high degree of standardisation.

Competition is mainly in price. To some extent competing firms are able also to offer better delivery dates.

In Scandinavia, as well as in Austria and Switzerland, a growing tendency to purchase in EFTA countries is noticeable. Steps taken to adjust to this situation include: changes in sales organisation, working agreements with foreign firms, and rationalisation within the firm. These adjustment measures apply both to EEC and to EFTA countries.

3. SEMI-FINISHED METAL PRODUCTS

A substantial increase in competition is reported in the EEC area mainly by established French and Italian firms. Here too the different taxation treatment of exports has had disadvantageous effects on German firms. Other advantages of foreign firms are said to be lower labour costs and larger labour reserves.

The market position in EFTA countries is still considered good, although British competition has strengthened in Austria and Switzerland, as well as in Scandinavia.

Competition by Belgian, Dutch and French firms in nonferrous and semi-finished metals is growing on the German market, as well as in Belgium/Luxemburg. Competitors do not offer higher quality; their prices are said to be due to hidden subsidies. Further details could not be obtained.

4. THE ELECTRICAL INDUSTRY

A manufacturer of high frequency installations reports that his market position in certain products has remained the same, competition not having altered significantly. He continues to export more to EFTA than to EEC countries. His main clients are public authorities, with whom his trade relations are long established. In other products he is co-operating with partners both within and without the Common Market area.

Competition in valves in the Italian market has greatly increased. Sales to Italy have declined, partly for this reason, and partly because of the prohibitively high custom duties. Subsidiaries of American firms are the main competitors in Italy.

In Britain, the prohibitively high import duties which protect the British valve cartel are unlikely to be reduced immediately. German firms are likely to continue to experience difficulties for a considerable time. Sales possibilities for radio and television valves in other EFTA countries are limited partly by quota restrictions. The existing customs discrimination strengthens the desire of users to purchase in their own countries. The sole measure for adjustment mentioned is enlargement of sales organisations.

5. ELECTRICAL HOUSEHOLD PRODUCTS

Competition in this field by Dutch, Belgian and Italian firms in the German market has increased considerably. Competition is mainly a matter of price. Foreign firms in particular have increased their sales promotion efforts. France has increased its supply of kitchen products, Italy of polishers, and the Dutch of vacuum cleaners.

By contrast, market conditions have not altered significantly in EFTA countries. Prospects are considered to be favourable where it is possible to extend service and sales organisations through existing subsidiaries.

6. VEHICLE CONSTRUCTION

Due to reduction in EFTA tariffs, British and Swedish firms have increased competitive pressure in Scandinavia. There is no intention as yet to change production so as to adjust to increased competition.

Tractor manufacturers complain about high import duties

in EEC countries, particularly Italy, where an import turn-over tax has over-compensated for reductions in tariffs.

Competition in the German market by Italian and French firms has increased. As a result there is considerable pressure on prices. Further reductions in custom and quota restrictions in EEC countries will, it is hoped, improve business.

7. VEHICLE COMPONENTS

Competition has increased sharply in the EEC area. Italy is a new competitor. Competition in sparking plugs extends more particularly to prices—subsidies are suspected—rather than to quality. On the other hand, the United States and Britain are increasing their supplies to the European market. The low prices of these offers arise through elimination of discounts. Measures of adjustment include intensification of market observation and extension of service. They apply to EEC as well as to EFTA countries.

8. TEXTILES

The German textile industry has suffered most severely in the home market from competition from EEC partners, as well as from other countries. The market structure has changed both in the Community and in EFTA. Increasing internal costs and up-valuation of the D-mark have accelerated structural changes.

Within the Community, Italy, France, Belgium and Holland are particularly strong competitors in partner countries, as well as in Germany.

It is stated that imports of unfinished materials from Japan are an important factor contributing to low prices of Italian competitors. In ready-made articles for women's and men's wear, the Italians have the advantage that, in addition to low prices, they offer very fashionable products. France is increasingly supplying the more expensive garments.

The majority of firms do not attribute the adverse situation to competition from other EEC countries, although competitive pressure from these countries has increased mainly because of differential taxation. To an increasing degree the supply position is affected by competition from Spanish, Portuguese and Swedish firms, as well as East European countries, Japan, Hong Kong and India. In addition to European competitors, the USA is competing in corsets and associated products. The sales effort by American firms with factories in Europe is particularly noticeable.

The hemp industry states that the Common Market Treaty to date has proved wholly disadvantageous because its suppliers of raw materials within the EEC are at the same time its strongest competitors in finished products, particularly Holland, Belgium and France. Italy, which had been the main supplier of raw materials, has ceased exports completely due to growing internal demand. The low prices offered by competitors could be explained partly by public subsidies. In some instances, these selling prices lie below German manufacturing costs, and could not be equalled whatever the rationalisation measures of the German hemp industry.

For the textile industry, sales possibilities in EFTA countries have generally deteriorated. EFTA markets could be held only in special products, designed to meet the tastes of the respective countries, and in those instances where long-established sales organisations help to further sales. Customs discrimination—the difference between Common Market and EFTA tariffs for woven fabrics is now about 6 per cent—is having a gradual, but very substantial, adverse effect on cotton spinning and weaving products. In addition, new suppliers are appearing in EFTA countries. In Scandinavia, for example, Austrian exports have increased.

EFTA regulations regarding origin have proved particularly disadvantageous to textile products. This applies to the weaving, as well as to the finishing, sector of the textile industry. Certain finishing orders from Switzerland could not be accepted due to the regulations governing origin. Business connections dating back for many years, for example in ribbon finishing, had to be broken. The cotton textile industry states that, in general, the increasing costs of its exports due to the up-valuation of the D-mark could not be compensated by reductions in the costs of imported raw materials.

Adjustment measures include strengthening market observation, co-operation with partners in EEC countries, increased purchases of semi-finished products within the Community and other countries, and extension of sales organisations. Within firms, production changes reflect in part increasing stress on high-quality and fashionable products, and in part increasing variety.

9. JEWELLERY, WATCHES AND CLOCKS

Competition within the Common Market area, including the German market, has considerably increased, particularly in inexpensive watches and simple jewellery. The reasons given for Italy's strong position in this field were lower wages. No particular reasons were mentioned with regard to France, which is increasing its offers.

In the EFTA countries, the market position has deteriorated in a similar way as for textiles. Markets could be maintained in special products and by paying particular regard to taste. The industry is not prepared to say whether these measures can be successful in view of the increasing tariff discrimination. Intensive market observation, increased sales promotion and changes in production, particularly in jewellery, are mentioned as measures of adjustment.

10. FOODSTUFFS

The different price levels for agricultural products and different subsidy payments affect the German food industry considerably.

It is stated that subsidies for exported French skimmed dried milk powder are higher than the price level on the French market. Dutch and Belgian firms are also offering products at prices with which the German industry cannot compete.

Price competition in German markets is strong in bakery and brewery products. Cheaper offers from EEC countries are made possible by purchases of raw materials at world prices. Manufacturers of spirits report that French, Italian and Dutch competitors have been favoured one-sidedly by the reduction in inter-Community tariffs. The flour-milling industry expressed apprehension in view of Germany's future agricultural policy as a member of the Common Market. Its situation has deteriorated through the return of the Saar to the Federal Republic.

The German food industry is unable to expand within the Common Market area partly because of the high German price level. Adjustment measures include increased co-operation with and licensing of firms in other EEC countries.

11. CHEMICAL INDUSTRY AND PHARMACEUTICAL PRODUCTS

Chemical firms in general report a deterioration in their market position, not only in the German market, but partly also in Belgium and Holland. However, firms manufacturing pharmaceutical specialities in particular have been able to maintain their position. France, Italy and also Belgium and Holland are new suppliers. Competitors in general offer more favourable prices. These lower prices are believed to be due to more favourable freight charges, lower material and energy costs, and above all lower wages. Lower production costs are therefore possible. Some competitors enjoy greater capital strength and fully utilise this advantage.

Firms producing specialities are able to maintain their position in EFTA markets. This applies especially to the pharmaceutical industry, which controls very effective sales organisations and qualified services in some EFTA countries. Long-established products are able to maintain their position even under changed conditions.

The chemical industry, on the other hand, states that difficulties in EFTA markets are increasing. Customs tariff discrimination, and also the tendency of many previous customers to purchase in other EFTA countries, is the principle cause of complaints. In addition Britain is undertaking large-scale production in certain products and its competition is becoming more effective in EFTA markets.

Decisive changes in manufacture have not yet occurred. It has become necessary, however, to increase marketing effort partly by increasing market research and sales promotion, and also by participating in more trade fairs.

Large firms having factories available in various European countries have to some extent shifted production to their subsidiaries to reduce costs. Should the rift between the Common Market countries and EFTA increase in the future, then such arrangements would have to take account of the regional split up of the European market. It is feared that the economics of overall production would suffer. A European solution to the integration problem is therefore considered essential.

12. BUILDING AND CONSTRUCTIONAL INDUSTRY

Transport costs are a specially important factor in the building and constructional industry. Nevertheless competition in German markets has increased. French brick manufacturers in particular are competing actively. Their strong position is due partly to quality, and partly to favourable prices based on lower wages, lower coal costs and above all on the French taxation system. German brick manufacturers are trying to remain competitive through increased rationalisation, but new methods in manufacture or sales are little in evidence.

Switzerland is the only potential market within EFTA for these industries. Due to prohibitive tariffs and the cartelisation of the Swiss constructional industry, the German industry to date has succeeded to only a limited extent in penetrating the Swiss market. On the other hand, Swiss contractors are very active on the German market.

13. LEATHER, PAPER, FURNITURE AND WOODWORKING INDUSTRIES

The reports are similar: increased competition in the EEC area and within EFTA; above all price competition, except in special products. Adjustment measures include: the extension of sales organisations, co-operation with foreign partners and reductions in range of products.

C. EVALUATION OF ADJUSTMENT MEASURES

The measures taken by German firms to adjust to the Common Market cannot be compared directly—although this has been attempted—with those of French or Italian firms. The original position must also be investigated and considered in relation to the actions taken.

German industry and trade policies since the end of the war have aimed at full integration of the German economy into the world economy. Regional objectives within the framework of the OEEC, for example, have been substantially subordinated to this larger purpose. Multilateral measures and treaties replaced bilateral trade and payment agreements and the D-mark was made more convertible relative to the currencies of the other OEEC countries. The Federal Republic engaged to a much lesser extent than other European countries in trade based on bilateral exchange of products with specific economic areas. Export guarantees did not seek specifically to cover risks with particular currency areas; for example, the dollar-drive risks.

The flow of product and capital responded to the world-wide orientation of German economic and trade policy. Consequently, at the time of the formation of the Common Market, about one-third of German exports were directed to Common Market countries, another third to other European countries including EFTA, and the remainder overseas. The direction of trade has scarcely altered since the formation of the Common

Market in spite of a rapid increase in volume due to the entirely different basic position of the other Common Market partners.

Only in the Netherlands were conditions similar to those in the Federal Republic. Italian and Belgian trade policies had been directed far more to OEEC countries on the one hand, and to the United States on the other, Belgium concentrating more on the American market than Italy. French industry found its main field of activity in the home market or in French overseas territories. Similarly France was by far the largest importer of the products of the *Communauté Française*. The dollar shortage encouraged a dollar export policy to increase hard currency earnings.

The French economy turned to the European market only because of the increasing tendency towards political and economic independence in their overseas possessions. This factor undoubtedly greatly encouraged French participation in the European economy. The formation of a large but self-contained Common Market corresponded far more to traditional French views than a world-wide orientation of trading policy or a liberal free trade area as favoured by Britain, which itself was based largely on concepts underlying the Commonwealth structure. It may indeed be much easier to change the direction of an economy from one market to another, as illustrated by the French example, than to concentrate on to one market an economy orientated to world-wide sales and imports, such as the German or the Dutch.

From another point of view, too, the formation of the Common Market has affected Germany's Common Market partners more favourably than Germany. In view of the favourable balance of payments in the Federal Republic, itself the result of an economic trade policy directed to world-wide exports, the quota restrictions of the Federal Republic were substantially less and tariffs were lower than corresponding restrictions and tariffs in France and Italy.

These two latter countries were able, therefore, to increase their exports to Germany substantially when German tariffs were further reduced from their already low level. The German effort in the opposite direction, by contrast, suffered from a time difference since French and Italian tariffs and quota restrictions started from a very much higher level and had to be correspondingly much further reduced before exports to these countries became attractive. The absolute level of these tariffs is still substantial in spite of the same proportionate reduction, with correspondingly adverse affects on German exports.

In view of the very liberal German laws governing domicile, a large number of French and Italian firms have established sales subsidiaries in the Federal Republic. In contrast, it may take up to one year to acquire a *carte de commerçant* for establishing a German subsidiary in France.

The fact that the first effective measures of the Common Market Treaty dealt with tariffs and quotas further favoured the other partners. The Federal Republic, in line with the world-wide orientation of its trade policy, has led in these fields. Other measures, by contrast, have been postponed due to the lack of a timetable in the Treaty. This applies particularly to harmonisation of taxation. Some partners partially compensate any reduction in custom duties by increasing the tax element to a level equivalent to the internal turnover tax. The turnover tax on internal products, however, is not always effective. Because of boom conditions, the Federal Republic did not use such tax adjustments, though this would have solved part of the problem. In France the very high turnover tax, which is recoverable *in toto* for exports, but is imposed with full vigour on imports, has three important consequences:

1. French producers can offer their products on the German market at a lower price than German manufacturers.

2. As selling price determines to some extent the size of the market, the high level of turnover tax in France reduces the market for German products, so that, in relation to population, the market is much smaller than, for example, the Dutch market.

3. The turnover tax on German products is only partly

refunded on exports to France, and therefore the German manufacturer is at some disadvantage in relation to the French producer in the French market.

The problem can be solved only by taking account also of direct taxation because of the different proportions of direct and indirect taxation in the total burden of competing firms in the various EEC countries. The greater the reduction of internal tariffs, the more important it is to the German economy for a solution of this problem to be found.

The various types, periods and degrees of trade cycle policies in EEC countries adversely affect competition and therefore German exports. For trade policy reasons, Holland has established a wage stabilisation policy, whereas in Germany wages continue to increase. In consequence, certain Dutch products can be offered in the Federal Republic at a price about one-third lower than that of corresponding German products. Certain Dutch producers have suggested to German manufacturers that the Germans should yield the French market to the Dutch and in return they would agree to offer their products in the German market at the same price level as German producers.

Finally, substantial differences in market structure in the various Common Market countries are of importance. The pace-setter in imports of craft products in many countries is the department store. In France, for example, the department store is much less significant than in other countries, and subsidiaries of foreign stores are unable to strengthen their position due to the French laws of domicile. In consequence, sales of imported products have to pass through the retail trade which charges high margins. French public authorities have established lower margins for imported products than are customary in home trade. These measures, however, do not—as believed by the Common Market Commission—favour the foreign supplier immediately, but only when the break-through to the mass market is achieved. For the time being such measures tend to act restrictively.

The tendency of German manufacturers to extend rather than neglect markets in third countries, particularly in EFTA, does not indicate a lack of interest in the Common Market. It is rather a positive contribution because, by enlarging sales abroad, manufacturers side-step the increasing pressure of EEC competitors in the German market. This competition, mainly the result of rationalisation and automation, cannot be met fully by German manufacturers partly because of increasing wage costs and partly because of distortions of competitive strength.

The Working Committee of the Chamber of Industry and Commerce in Baden-Württemberg concludes that the reaction of German firms to the formation and development of the Common Market has been hardly less spontaneous and intensive than the reaction in other EEC countries. This applies at least to those market forces which have not been subjected to boom conditions. Due to their different starting points, the actions taken by German firms differ from those of Common Market partners. In the speed of the reaction to changing market conditions, German firms are probably in advance of German economic policy—*e.g.* tax harmonisation, right of domicile and cartel regulations.

II A Belgian Investigation

An extract from the report of the investigation carried out by the Chamber of Craft Industries, Brussels, is quoted here to illustrate the efforts of smaller countries in the Common Market.

To the question, "*Has your firm taken action to adjust to new competition, or is such action contemplated?*", affirmative replies were received under the following heads:

AFFIRMATIVE REPLIES

Changes in manufacture or sales programme   ..   163

Standardisation of products   109

Further development of distribution or manufacturing methods   182

Market research   134

Establishing contacts with firms in Common Market or EFTA countries   158

Joining a trade association   103

Joining an international trade association   91

Participating in foreign trade fairs   85

Establishing subsidiaries, sales offices, agencies, etc., in one or several countries of the Common Market or EFTA   53

Other measures   35

NO REPLY   130

To the question, "*Has your firm established contact with competing firms in order to improve its competitive strength?*", the following replies were received, divided according to the nationality of the firm approached:

BELGIAN FIRMS

No	268
Yes	98
No reply	106

EEC FIRMS

No	243
Yes	114
No reply	115

EFTA FIRMS

No	276
Yes	43
No reply	153

The *Chambre de Commerce de Bruxelles* comments on the replies of these questions:

"Taking account of the costs of new installations, etc., the measures taken by Belgian firms to adjust to the new situation can be considered as satisfactory.

"The fear that we would be unable to compete due to the dynamic enterprise of our powerful neighbour countries has proved unjustified.

"At present numerous negotiations are proceeding with the object of eventual co-operation above all with foreign firms, but only a few of these negotiations have achieved success. This probably reflects the relatively short period of the existence of the Common Market.

"It is to be regretted that, to date, only relatively few contacts have been established with other Belgian firms in spite of the advantages of combining with a view to specialisation. This would appear to be due, however, more to lack of knowledge of the possibilities than to lack of goodwill."

III The French Economy in the Common Market

The efforts of French industry for and within the Common Market are stressed here for the following three reasons. France and the Federal Republic have approximately the same population. Both countries suffered, although in different ways, through the Second World War. The experience of the French economy shows the success that can be achieved by a determined liberal foreign trade policy (since 1959), together with an imaginative and active spirit of enterprise. A particularly thorough study of France's efforts in this field is contained in the *Bottin Europe*, published by the Société Didot-Bottin, 1 rue Sébastien Bottin, Paris VII.

A. THE ECONOMIC PLAN

Economic planning provided the basis of French industry's preparation for the Common Market. The Third Economic Plan of 1958–1961 was particularly important; its objective was the European orientation of French firms. The present Fourth Plan serves the same purpose, namely, to adjust the French economy fully to the European Community. These Economic Plans must be seen in conjunction with the consolidation achieved by Pinay and Rueff. Their main achievements were:

1. Reduction in public subsidies (50 per cent reduction).

2. Liberalisation of imports.

3. Devaluation by 17·5 per cent.

The individual Plans were successful, although the Third Plan in particular was endangered by political events, notably the war in Algeria.

Irrespective of political and economic views, French firms consider it almost a natural right, and the state regards it as a public duty, for industry to be supported by the public authorities.

Some of the actions of the public authorities deserve to be mentioned. The most important action has been the elimination of turnover tax on exports. In consequence, turnover tax has become an important factor in the success of French products abroad and in particular in Common Market countries. Subsidies for modernisation, rationalisation and factory transfers completed the range of classical means of export assistance.

Also relevant is the publicity effort to promote the EEC directed by the public information service, the *Centre National du Commerce Extérieur*, Paris, which corresponds to the Federal Office of Information Services in Cologne. German visitors to EEC functions organised by France frequently express surprise at the scale of resources available in France for such purposes. Although detailed information on the sums involved is not available, considerable public expense for Common Market information purposes has been and is being incurred in France. The opportunities available for establishing co-operatives of firms backed by government aid should also be noted. In particular, when co-operatives are formed of small and medium-sized firms, each having up to 500 employees and with a capital of not more than 5 million N.F., the effect is to stimulate exports. Some of the existing agreements of this type—about 50—admittedly are directed solely at rationalisation, specialisation and combined production, but success in achieving these objectives creates a new need for markets, and exports become essential. In consequence production co-operatives tend in time to become sales co-operatives. This possibility has been realised by a number of firms not only within but also outside these government-supported associations. Finally, the facilities offered for export credit insurance and market research insurance should be mentioned. The latter in particular guarantees to home producers that capital needed for opening up foreign markets—for example, expenses in market research, as well as in establishing subsidiaries and in sales promotion—shall be recoverable in case of partial or complete failure, except for a small proportion borne by the firm.

One further French activity justifies consideration: the use of commercial advisers (*conseillers commerciaux*) who are attached to various industrial centres in foreign states and are controlled by the respective ambassadors. In addition to reports to their Government, these commercial advisers inform their compatriots on local, industrial and business conditions, and introduce them to public authorities and representatives of industry.

B. INDUSTRIAL ACTIVITY

French industry in almost all its component parts, and to a greater degree than industry in any other EEC country, opposed the Common Market at the time of the discussions which led to the Treaty of Rome. After the Common Market became established, French industrialists not only accepted the position, but they showed an extraordinary activity in utilising the opportunities of the European "adventure".

I PREPARATION: MARKET RESEARCH

Intensive study of information about EEC countries, including numerous requests to the official Franco-German Chamber of Commerce for data, was followed by very vigorous activity in market observation and research. Two approaches to market investigations were notable. First, industrialists and their colleagues travelled in the country under investigation; secondly, market research institutes were utilised. These latter specialised increasingly after 1959 in investigations in EEC countries. In numerous cases both methods were used. It is not exaggerating to say that large groups systematically visited specific Common Market countries or specific economic areas, and thoroughly investigated all the possibilities, latent and apparent. The support by France's official representatives in these various countries proved its value. A remarkable development followed. Investigation of foreign markets, utilising market research institutes, became a normal part of the approach of industry, irrespective of sector or size.

II INTERNAL AND EXTERNAL ADJUSTMENT PROCESSES

Within firms, the decisions based on the results of market research led to rationalisation, modernisation and specialisation. The required capital was obtained by means of internal savings, amalgamations and concentration of production. Mainly French capital was used. The following industrial sectors were particularly active:

> Chemical industry
> Machine industry
> Electrical industry
> Food industry
> Textile industry
> Iron and steel industries
> Paper industry
> Vehicle and aircraft industries
> Banking and insurance
> Ceramics

At the same time, co-operation in its most extensive and various forms developed. According to a statement made by the Director-General of the *Deutsche Industrie-und Handelstag,* Dr. Düren, the Common Market encouraged about twice as much concentrated activity in French as in German industry. Those activities, which should prove most instructive, can be summarised as follows:

1. Establishing co-operative research institutes.

2. Licensing arrangements.

3. Establishing co-operative finance organisations to facilitate loans.

French newspapers, periodicals and economic information services report agreements between firms almost daily. These agreements are noticeably more frequent with other Common Market firms than with home (*i.e.* French) firms. It is naturally of interest to indicate the more active sectors. A complete tabulation would be extremely difficult, but the most important are the following:

> Machine industry
> Chemical industry
> Electrical industry
> Vehicle and aircraft construction
> Banking and insurance
> Energy supply industry
> Food industry
> Consultant engineers
> Textile industry

III COMMERCIAL ACTIVITY

The preparatory moves in anticipation of the Common Market included search for data on demographic conditions, user habits and price structure in potential markets abroad. The following methods were used:

1. Questions addressed to internal and foreign official organisations, in particular Chambers of Industry and Commerce.

2. Fact-finding missions by managers and co-workers to Common Market countries.

3. Procurement of competitive products.

4. Commissioning market research institutes.

The intensity of French commercial activity, and, at the same time, a certain lack of experience, are indicated by the submission, in some instances, of questionnaires requesting information to hotel guests and even to friends and relations of business men.

Naturally, the prospects for the penetration of other Common Market countries by commercial organisations are more limited. It would appear that few subsidiaries or branch offices have been established except, of course, by department stores whose international connections are well known.

(a) GENERAL EXAMPLES

As a rule, French commercial firms seek direct contact with EEC customers. Direct contacts are established by German-speaking French agents or by visits. Frequently general agents are used. This has the advantage of utilising already existing and well-established agency networks. Agencies also offer the substantial advantage that they are able to deal with customs and import formalities which are particularly important for consumer goods.

An interesting recent development is exchange of products. A French trader sells the product of his partner in France in return for the sale of his own product by his partner abroad. In these cases, the general agent frequently turns to exporting on his own account.

International co-operation by department stores preceded the formation of the Common Market. Numerous new developments, however, are noticeable since the formation of the EEC. Previously, contacts were established mainly through visits by salesmen or purchasers. Now numerous purchasing and sales offices have been set up which report to their main offices on fluctuations in markets and changes in consumer behaviour, and are able to accept particularly favourable offers immediately.

Two especially instructive examples are cited here to illustrate French activity in the sales of branded articles. Eight French food-manufacturing companies formed an organisation in North-Rhine-Westphalia as early as the summer of 1958, *i.e.* immediately after the Common Market agreements. The aims of the organisation are to establish business connections between French firms manufacturing branded food products and German wholesalers; more specifically the organisation seeks to import and export, to act as an agency and wholesaler for French branded products, especially food products and other articles in daily use. An office, including an exhibition hall, was established. The German-speaking manager became particularly active in market research and observation, in opening up markets and in public relations. Public relations included the placing of articles in the press which stressed the excellence of French cooking, making hidden references to the branded products sold by the firm. With this went invitations to restaurateurs, hotel managers and bar keepers to sample food and drinks. Last, but not least, contacts were made with wholesalers, consumer co-operatives and the more important hotels.

The success of this endeavour varied for individual products, but at all events it established the practicability of enlarging the market from specialised grocery shops to more general food stores and particularly to supermarkets which are accessible to the main mass of consumers. The various trade fairs, such as the cheese and wine samplings arranged by the French exhibitors, complement those efforts.

(b) EXAMPLE OF SOPEXA

The *Handelsblatt* reported on 29th January 1962 the formation of a French Information Office called SOPEXA (*Société pour la Promotion des Exports Alimentaires*) to assist exports of French food products to the Federal Republic. This company, which is registered as a private company, but is financed by the French state, will be engaged in the first instance in the sales promotion of French cheeses. North-Rhine-Westphalia has been selected as a test area in view of its purchasing power and favourable transport position. The office which acts for the "Association of Promoters of French Cheeses" seeks in the first instance to advise the wholesale and retail trade, and generally to nurse the market. In addition to placing advertisements in trade papers, SOPEXA has conducted an advertising campaign since 10th March 1962, utilising supplements in daily papers, showing publicity films (March and April) in 36 cinemas in North-Rhine-Westphalia, as well as in the adjacent areas of Hessen, Saarland and Rhineland-Palatinate, and sponsoring "commercials" on Radio Luxemburg. A widely based advertising campaign is proposed for the autumn.

Representatives of SOPEXA stated at a meeting in Düsseldorf that consumption of cheese per head in the Federal Republic grew from 2·7 to 4·5 kilograms between 1950 and 1960, and can with confidence be expected to expand further. In 1960, imports contributed about 101,000 tons to a total consumption of 250,000 tons. SOPEXA hopes to increase the percentage of French cheese imports to Germany in competition with Dutch and Italian products, particularly as consumption expands. Sales effort concentrates in the first instance on eight types of cheeses, which may meet, amongst others, the requirement of German consumers worried about their figures. SOPEXA states that in the provinces about 280 different sorts and types of cheeses are manufactured in France. It is of interest that wine has not been included (at least for the time being) in sales efforts, in contrast, for example, to the sales weeks ("France invites you to her table") held in 1959 in Hamburg, Düsseldorf and Dortmund. Importers point to German beer consumption as one reason, and also to the desire to remove from French cheeses the "stigma" of being a luxury product so as to establish a new mass market.

(c) WORK OF INSEAD

All France's Common Market partners rightly stress French activity in the training and further education of its business men. All organisations or associations of any importance in France organise seminars on Common Market topics. An example of the intensive effort made by the French economy to arouse interest in Common Market topics was the study meeting arranged in December 1961 by the *Euro-Economie* in association with INSEAD sponsored, amongst others, by the periodicals *Handelsblatt* and the *Betriebsberater*. (*Euro-Economie* is an association founded in Paris in 1961 which seeks, together with similar bodies in other countries, to harmonise the methods of European industry. In the Federal Republic *Euro-Economie* co-operates with the *Deutsche Gesellschaft für Betriebswirtschaft*.)

The two-day meeting aimed at acquainting French firms with the existing market position in Europe, with particular reference to the German market. The following subjects were dealt with:

1. The system of retaining title to property rights in the Federal Republic.

2. Methods of exploiting the German market.

3. Habits of German consumers: taste, requirements, purchasing power.

4. The German customs system.

5. German foreign trade.

The *Institut Européen d'Administration d'Affaires* (INSEAD) at Fontainebleau has shown notable activity in training European business managers. This Institute for Management Training is open to post-graduates of EEC countries and all European countries. The method of teaching is based on case histories, as practised particularly by the Business School of Harvard University. Students are encouraged to solve particularly difficult cases on the basis of actual European examples, such as require solution by managers within the Common Market. The mixture of instructors and students from all parts of Europe, the international subject matter and the case histories should facilitate the training of a new European business leadership. The results to date have not been unsatisfactory.

C. THE COMMON MARKET AS A TURNING POINT FOR FRENCH INDUSTRY

This short description of the French activities in the Common Market clearly shows that France offers an example of the successful utilisation of possibilities in the Common Market area. It behoves her partners to study these various activities to see whether they can be copied.

A comparison between the efforts made by the French economy and those of other Common Market countries is particularly favourable to France. But two factors must be mentioned which have favoured intensive and comprehensive Common Market activity by France. On the one hand, the Common Market made it absolutely imperative for French industry to overcome its partial stagnation; on the other hand, the overtly liberal direction of France's foreign trade policy formed an essential basis for progress. It cannot be doubted, however, that the turning point for France in becoming a successful exporter and a modern industrial power was the establishment of the Common Market.

PART III

ASPECTS OF THE COMMON MARKET TREATY RELEVANT TO BUSINESS ACTIVITY

ASPECTS OF THE COMMON MARKET TREATY RELEVANT TO BUSINESS ACTIVITY

I Regional Policy

One of the main aspects of the Common Market Treaty is its regional policy. Regional policy is a particular form of economic policy and concentrates on a *regio*, a specific economic area, and seeks its development. The preamble of the Treaty states that there should be a balanced development of different economic areas. The regional policy of the EEC will gain in importance as member-states of the Common Market, considered as separate closed economic units, lose their importance —an inescapable development of the realisation of the Treaty. At present, a purely European regional policy, based solely on the EEC Community, is not possible. The structure of the individual economies in the Common Market is too different. In size, wealth and capacity and in their economic and location policies, member-states vary too greatly. Therefore at present the regional policy of member-states is still a national policy.

The Treaty states in *Article 92*, albeit indirectly, that subsidies—generally considered to distort competition—are compatible with the Common Market provided that they further the economic development of areas in which living standards are exceptionally low or in which unemployment is heavy. It is certain that a specific EEC regional policy will be introduced in addition to harmonising the regional policies of the individual member-states. This policy will be one of the most important consequences of the Treaty of Rome and will have a significant impact on individual firms.

A. RELEVANT POINTS IN THE TREATY

One point of particular interest to industry with regard to regional policy is contained in *Article 42* of the Treaty. This states that the Council of Ministers may permit subsidies within the framework of an economic development program in the agricultural sector. According to *Article 43*, the European Fund—still to be formed—should promote, through limited financial aid, adjustments in the agricultural structure of individual countries.

Regional policy also affects transport regulations. *Article 80* of the Treaty states that the Commission during the current second transitional stage may investigate freight and transportation regulations in a member-state and establish whether these assist or protect one or several specific firms or industries. This power can be exercised either at the initiative of the Commission or at the request of a member-state. The investigation is intended to establish whether these aids distort competition.

The regulations governing the European Investment Bank also state that one of the tasks of this organisation shall be to facilitate a balanced and friction-free development of the Common Market. The European Investment Bank, a non-profit-making institution, facilitates the financing of enterprises in less developed areas by means of loans or guarantees (*Article 130* of the Treaty). The European Investment Bank is considered in more detail at a later stage (pp. 140–142).

B. SPECIAL REGULATIONS FOR CERTAIN AREAS

Special regulations govern the regional policy of Italy, Berlin and the border areas adjacent to Eastern Germany. In addition, temporary regulations, operative during the transition period, permit, by agreement with the EEC authorities, the employment of protective measures in case of economic difficulties in certain regions.

In a further protocol, the member-states of the Community recognise the development program for Southern Italy and the Italian islands. They recommend that special assistance should be made available by the European Investment Bank and European Social Fund. Italy in consequence will enjoy a privileged position in applying for assistance from these institutions and applications in the spirit of this protocol are likely to be granted.

Of particular importance to Western Germany is the acceptance by all governments of the Community, as agreed during the conference on the Common Market and Euratom, of the obligation to take suitable actions to ease the economic situation of Berlin, promote its development and maintain its industrial stability. In addition subsidies are permissible in certain areas of the Federal Republic to compensate for adverse effects arising from the partition of Germany.

C. THE FIRST EEC REGIONAL POLICY CONFERENCE

The first Regional Policy Conference met in Brussels in December 1961 and was attended by 200 experts, representing the relevant organisations—governmental agencies, Chambers of Commerce, and administrative, scientific and industrial bodies. German industry was represented by the *Deutsche Industrie-und Handelstag* and some specially interested Chambers of Industry and Commerce. The Conference had as its objects:

1. To establish the closest possible contact between the people of the six Common Market countries responsible for the formation and execution of regional policy.

2. To learn from the experience gained by the six countries so as to facilitate a balanced development of the large regions which make up individual national economies.

3. To indicate the aspects of regional problems which are of common interest (including the effect of the Common Market on these problems and their possible solutions).

4. To advise governments and the Commission on the basic principles of regional policy and to consider and evaluate the kind of support the Commission can offer to member-states in this field.

The topics of discussion outlined below provide an interesting survey of the most important points of European regional policy.

I REGIONAL QUESTIONS

1. GERMAN FEDERAL REPUBLIC

(i) "The problems arising in peripheral areas from the labour market point of view as illustrated by the example of Schleswig-Holstein."

(ii) "The Emsland programme and the integrated development of an agrarian border area of the Federal Republic."

(iii) "Development in an economically weak region as illustrated by the example of Eifel-Hunsrück."

(iv) "Problems of a peripheral industrial area taking account particularly of zonal border difficulties, as illustrated by the example of Oberfranken."

(v) "The development programme for central localities in structurally weak rural areas of the Federal Republic."

2. FRANCE

(i) "The example 'Bas-Rhône-Languedoc' and the programme of regional action."

(ii) "Structural changes, the flight from the land and economic developments in Western France."

(iii) "Co-operation of public and private enterprise in the development of an industrial centre—the Lacq example."

(iv) "Equipment companies and infrastructure in different industrial areas in France."

(v) "Participation by regional research institutes in the preparation and execution of regional programmes."

3. ITALY

   (i) "Reclamation, soil improvement and irrigation within the framework of the development programme of the Mezzogiorno."

   (ii) "Problems of labour supply and vocational training in the Mezzogiorno."

   (iii) "The method of intervention by public bodies and the role of the *Cassa per il Mezzogiorno* (Development Fund for Southern Italy)."

4. BELGIUM

   (i) "Problems and perspectives of Belgian border areas."

   (ii) "Industrial adjustment in a declining Belgian region."

5. NETHERLANDS

"Regional planning and co-ordination in local, industrial, agricultural, cultural and social sectors in Dutch regional development."

6. GENERAL QUESTIONS AND FRONTIER REGIONS

   (i) "Some aspects of a firm's growth within the framework of regional development."

   (ii) "Harmonising the development of two frontier areas —Belgian South Luxemburg and French North Lorraine."

   (iii) "Problems and perspectives of a border area in the centre of the Community."

II RESULTS OF CONFERENCE

The results of the EEC's first Regional Policy Conference can be summarised as follows:

The Conference showed the need for an adequate and appropriate regional policy. A rapid and global expansion of the European economy cannot be maintained without an effective regional policy since the rate of further growth in areas already in advanced development will necessarily decline. The rhythm of progress—as shown by the example of the United States—slows down after a time. To maintain the desired growth of average productivity in the Community, the growth of the less developed areas must be accelerated.

The following four regional problems arise within the Common Market:

1. The underdevelopment of an area of low agricultural productivity and open or hidden structural unemployment (particularly Southern Italy).

2. The decay of certain industrial areas due to a decline in their predominant industries (textiles, coal, etc.). In such cases diversification is essential.

3. Excessive concentration in certain areas requiring a more than proportional increase in infrastructure and services with consequent social disadvantages. Here the problem is one of decentralisation.

4. The artificial division of certain natural economic areas and zones due to national frontiers.

The Conference considered the measures which have solved or which are intended to solve these problems. It made a special study of the more typical cases. The experiences of member-states were then compared.

The most important results can be outlined as follows:

1. Regional policy must be strengthened in border areas of the Community.

2. The interdependence of structural improvements in agriculture and industrialisation is acknowledged. Industry should be attracted to the sources of labour supply. This would reduce to reasonable limits the need for emigration to distant industrial centres either at home or abroad by workers from agricultural areas. In Southern Italy in particular a population reserve should be maintained to facilitate local industrialisation.

3. Factors relevant to the process of industrialisation.

   (a) The first steps in the industrialisation of agrarian development areas should be the establishment of industries processing agricultural products in specific chosen localities. These would attract other industries. The view that industry should be attracted to selected central localities was generally accepted. Only in the special case of Germany's border zones would assistance be provided on a broad basis.

   (b) The improvement of infrastructure is of primary importance. Only if the attraction of improved infrastructure is inadequate can temporary assistance be justified to firms willing to settle.

   (c) The development of a social infrastructure is also necessary (housing, schools, recreational facilities, etc.). These should not be neglected in relation to the infrastructure covering energy, transport and water supply.

   (d) Vocational training purposefully directed must be encouraged as a prerequisite to industrialisation of these development centres. Vocational training efforts directed to certain regions should not, however, affect the liberty of movement of workers within the EEC area, and should not undermine the guiding principles established by the EEC Commission for the training of employees and their teachers.

4. The choice of these central industrial settlements should be limited to towns of about 50,000 inhabitants which are able and willing to develop and act as centres of attraction. (In especially underdeveloped areas, towns of 20–30,000 inhabitants may be eligible.) The selection and development of central nuclei villages to maintain agricultural population does not appear necessary. Agriculture would benefit from the industrial centres.

Further investigations by the EEC Commission will consider the following particular problems:

  (i) Peripheral regions and zonal border areas.

 (ii) Decentralisation or concentration in establishing new industries.

(iii) The type and extent of permissible government help for regional development.

(iv) Potential dangers to competition of special methods of support for regional areas.

 (v) The possibilities of exchanging and utilising the national experiences of EEC countries. All member states and firms should be informed of the experiences of neighbouring countries.

(vi) Problems of transportation and their regional aspects.

(vii) The formation of European industrial centres as development centres of the Community.

II Free Movement of Labour

On 26th August 1961, Regulation no. 15 was published "on the first steps to establish free movement of labour within the Community". (*Official Journal* of the same date.)

This regulation is based on the directive that all differences in the treatment of employees in member-states in respect of employment, remuneration or other matters governed by nationality, are to be eliminated not later than the end of the transition period, *i.e.* by 31st December 1969. The right of individuals to free movement may be limited only for reasons of public security, safety or health. These rights include specifically:

1. The right to apply for positions actually offered and to have unhindered access and freedom of movement within member-states for this purpose;

2. the right of the individual to live in member-states and carry out his occupation according to current laws and regulations.

Article 49 of the Rome Treaty lists the prerequisites to be established to obtain the objects laid down in *Article 48*. *Article 48* in particular requires:

(i) close co-operation between the national labour administrations;

(ii) progressive elimination of administrative measures and acts and time limits imposed in connection with available employment opportunities and which hinder free movement of employees;

(iii) progressive elimination of all time-limits and other limitations in job opportunities which impose conditions on employees from other EEC states which differ from the conditions imposed on employees of the home state;

(iv) suitable provisions for equalising supply and demand in the labour market under conditions which exclude any danger to living standards and employment levels in individual areas and industries.

A. STAGES IN ESTABLISHING FREEDOM OF MOVEMENT

Article 49 of the EEC Treaty stipulates that freedom of movement should be established progressively. The Commission's regulations cover the first stage only. In a commentary to the regulations it has, however, indicated in broad outline the progress required during the later stages, and this commentary forms the basis for interpreting individual provisions. It is proposed that, in the second period, preferences for home labour should be restricted and be operative only in exceptional cases. In addition the Commission in these regulations affirms its intention of assisting in balancing labour supply and demand by strengthening co-operation between the relevant authorities in the respective national labour administrations. During the third period, considered as the end phase, any difficulties remaining will be dealt with and the obstacles restricting movement of employees will be eliminated. In consequence, at the end of the transition period, wage and salary conditions within the area of every member-state will be the same for all nationals of the Community.

B. ACTION DURING THE FIRST STAGE

The declaration of the Council of Ministers on the speeding up of the process of integration (June 1960) specifically mentions freedom of movement. Taking account of this declaration, the regulations state that the first period is limited to two years and will end in August 1963.

During this period nationals of the home state will have priority. Jobs may be reserved for such labour for a period of up to three weeks. For occupations suffering from labour shortage, to be listed periodically on a regional basis, employment permission should be freely available. Equally, an employer specifying workers by name will be able to employ these irrespective of the condition of the local labour market, provided that certain occupational and family provisions of the regulations have been met.

To approximate more closely to an optimum degree of employment within the Community, it has been accepted as reasonable that the unemployed of member-states of the Community should have priority over employees from countries outside the Community. Accordingly the regulations include a provision that member-states should seek to ensure that vacancies not offered to named persons should be offered to employees from the Community.

The regulations also guarantee the same protection and treatment regarding conditions of work and employment opportunities. The same criteria as apply to the indigenous labour force in respect of the medical welfare and personal fitness and job-qualifications of employees, and all such similar requirements, must apply equally to employees from other member countries of the Community.

Finally, special regulations deal with wives and with children under age and with the employment of members of employees' families.

To ensure equal progress between member-states, the regulations have established the following framework:

    (i) An advisory committee consisting of an equal number of representatives of governments, employers and employees; and a technical committee of government representatives.

    (ii) An office to co-ordinate measures to balance supply and demand for labour for the Community as a whole. This office is to act as a clearing house, facilitating exchange of demand and supply in the labour market.

Special measures are proposed to accelerate vocational training of unskilled and inadequately skilled labour so as to improve their employment opportunities abroad.

The aim of these measures is to facilitate a better balance in the supply and demand of labour.

Within six months of the ratifications of the regulations, the Commission will work out proposals regarding seasonal workers and employees in frontier regions.

The following points are particularly relevant to firms employing foreign labour from EEC countries or firms which are considering doing so:

1. The correct approach to foreign labour is by means of the relevant employment exchanges.

2. After satisfactory employment for a period of one year, the foreign worker may claim prolongation of his employment permit for the same trade. (Interruptions in the one-year period are permissible up to a limit of 40 days per year for holidays, absence through illness, childbirth, accidents or occupational diseases.)

3. After satisfactory employment for a period of three years, the foreign worker is permitted to take jobs in other trades in which he has special skills at a corresponding wage or salary level.

4. After four years' satisfactory employment, he may undertake any job at the appropriate wage or salary level under the same conditions which apply to nationals.

5. On 30th September 1962 the Commission will submit to the Council of Ministers proposals for regulations covering the degree of liberalisation required during the second period.

6. To date, the regulations so far made to liberalise the Community's labour market have not had an exception-

ally strong impact. Subsequent regulations, however, will include more positive steps to simplify the formalities governing the free movement of labour. The regulations governing the Community's labour market are therefore of specific interest to industry.

III Domicile

The liberalisation of the rights of domicile made possible by the Rome Treaty aims at improving choice of locality to meet production requirements and at furthering a rational division of labour in the Common Market. It extends to:

1. Nationals of member-states and of their overseas possessions.

2. All companies which, according to the laws of member-states, their overseas areas or possessions, have their headquarters, their centres of administration or their principal units within the Community, or in overseas territories or possessions associated with it.

The Council of Ministers established on 25th October 1961 the first programme for removing restrictions on domicile and drew up timetables for making this liberalisation effective in various occupations.

The right of domicile accorded by the Rome Treaty is of much greater significance than rights arising from bilateral agreements on domicile. In general, the latter are a matter of special and exceptional privileges, though these may be quite extensive. The Treaty has, however, gone further and has established the fundamental principle of equality between all workers in the Community, both "native" and "foreign". In other words, any differences in treatment between nationals and the subjects of other member-states due to legal enactments or administrative regulations and practices are held to be restrictions of domicile.

Regulations on employment in individual member-states which do not take account of nationality are not affected. To obviate potential difficulties due to the multitude of legal and administrative regulations in the Community, it may be necessary to take special measures of co-ordination when limitations are being lifted. The general programme states that the fitness of such measures should be examined on the merits of each case. From this examination are excluded certain occupations specifically mentioned in the Treaty—insurance and pharmaceutical, medical and similar occupations—in which, according to the views of the Commission, co-ordination is required.

Activities connected with state authority, public order, safety and health in member-states are not affected by regulations on freedom of domicile.

The general programme, supplemented by an explanatory commentary, lays down the sequence of individual steps for eliminating discrimination. The guiding principle is embodied in *Article 54, paragraph 3* of the Treaty, and establishes preference for "activities where freedom of domicile would significantly further production and trade".

Accordingly, the majority of occupations in industry and trade will be liberalised before the end of the second year of the second period, *i.e.* before 31st December 1963. (Should the same activities be carried out by craftworkers, they will be liberalised just the same, but the interests of craftsmen will be safeguarded because the general programme's provisions for co-ordination are very elastic in their formulation.)

In addition to the economic criteria proposed in the Treaty, the plan will also take account of existing regulations which are of greater or lesser importance in individual states and might justify co-ordination measures before, during or after the lifting of restrictions. To facilitate the investigation of complex measures of co-ordination, it has been proposed that action in regard to certain particular sectors, such as insurance, be postponed to a date within the third period, *i.e.* between 1st January 1966 and 31st December 1967.

The rights of domicile, as applied to the transport industry, should become effective in the same way as for other industries.

The Commission has proposed that limitations on entrepreneurs in the field of transportion should be lifted before the end of the second year of the third period, and for the forwarding and removal agencies before the end of the second year of the second period.

The co-ordination of legal and administrative regulations proposed in *Article 57* indicates a substantial overlap between the regulations on rights of domicile and the Community's transport policy in regard to road and internal waterways transportation. This applies particularly to the examination of road traffic requirements (see the details of the programme for freedom of domicile in the *Official Journal of the European Community*, 15th January 1962.)

IV Free Movement in Service Industries

The Commission has submitted to the Council a general programme for lifting restrictions on free movement in service industries by methods similar to those governing domicile. (*Article 63, paragraph 1* of the Treaty.) This was approved by the Council of Ministers on 25th October 1961. The problem arises how to define service and restrictions on service, as well as the timetable for their abolition. Services are defined as:

> "services offered in return for payment insofar as they are not covered by the regulations on free movement of goods and capital and persons" (or are dealt with under transportation).

The Treaty is concerned here with the free movement of services within the Community; the person offering services must therefore be resident in a state of the Community other than the state receiving the service (*Article 49, paragraph 1*). A transfer of service across a frontier must therefore take place.

Three possibilities arise:

(a) A journey of the person providing the service to the person receiving the service. This applies to services of a professional nature in the widest sense—advisory, assessment, or technical services in industry, assembly, repair and maintenance of machinery, certain business services, trade representation, market research, client services, and rarer categories, such as handcraft and agricultural services which are confined to frontier regions. These categories of services are distinct from those involving domicile because in their case the productive activity in the other Common Market country is purely temporary.

(b) A journey of the person receiving the service to the person providing service. Such services include, for example, services received by the recipient during holidays abroad, or during visits for personal reasons to the member state (family visits or study), or as business representative, or for medical or similar treatment, or for other purposes.

(c) The transfer across the frontier of the service itself; both the recipient and the giver of the service remain in their own country. Either the service may be embodied in a product which is transferred (conversion processes, finishing and checking, investigations, analysis, etc.), or, alternatively, the physical base of the service may be transferred (certain services by banks, insurance companies, recruitment agencies and some professional services in the form of written work, transmission of information of all kinds, etc.).

The distinction between the concept of domicile and service is difficult only in cases involving frontiers, in which the person providing the service visits the country of the person receiving the service, and remains there for a period of time, or carries out a number of services. The Commission has established certain guiding principles. (See "Traffic in Services" published in *Official Journal of the European Community*, 15th January 1962.)

According to the Treaty (*Article 63, paragraph 3*), the priorities to be observed in eliminating restrictions are similar to those regarding domicile, but liberalisation will be more rapid.

However, it is important to remember that, according to *Article 61, paragraph 1*, the free movement of services in the transportation industry is to be realised through the common transport policy laid down in *Article 75 ff*. The general programme lifting restrictions on services does not cover transportation: special regulations are envisaged in *Article 75, paragraph 1 (a)* for eliminating restrictions in transportation service.

V Special EEC Credit Facilities

Large investments are needed to enable firms to meet the manifold tasks and opportunities arising from the unified European market. To meet these needs the authors of the Treaty of Rome established two European institutions, the European Investment Bank and the European Social Fund. The opportunities available in Germany of obtaining credit from the *Kreditanstalt für Wiederaufbau* (Federal Fund for Reconstruction) are outlined in Appendix V. The liberalisation of capital movement foreseen in the Treaty will further facilitate the flow of capital across national frontiers.

A. LIBERALISATION OF CAPITAL MOVEMENT BY STAGES

To facilitate the free interplay of forces in the capital markets of the Community, *Article 67* of the Treaty requires member states to eliminate progressively all restrictions on the movement of capital between their nationals during the transition period. In addition, all discriminatory measures are to be abolished which are based on the nationality or domicile of the parties or depend on the locality where investment takes place—at least to the extent needed for the proper functioning of the Common Market. Complete liberalisation is not yet insisted on. Under certain conditions, it is permissible to maintain and extend restrictions.

According to the directives to *Article 67* of the Rome Treaty (*Official Journal of the European Community*, 12th July 1960, page 91), liberalisation measures should include:

1. Free and irrevocable permission for transfers of foreign currencies, for business requirements including direct investment, and for the movement of "personal" capital (*i.e.* inheritances).

2. Facilitation of business activities involved in the purchase of securities dealt with on Stock Exchanges, subject, however, to the limitation that the purchase of foreign securities may be restricted to certain business sectors.

These guiding principles are not of great importance to the Federal Republic because capital movements have already been liberalised in West Germany. They apply mainly to France and Italy where capital movement is still subject to many restrictions.

B. THE EUROPEAN INVESTMENT BANK

A special European Bank has been founded, the *European Investment Bank*, to meet the large investment needs of regional policy and the adjustment of firms to the Common Market. Its legal basis was established according to *Articles 129* and *130* of the Treaty and "the protocol on the statutes of the European Investment Bank".

The European Investment Bank has an important role to play, both directly and indirectly, in regional planning policy. It finances investments to open up the less developed areas of member states.

The Bank also finances modernisation and adjustment activities by firms, thereby contributing to the solution of problems arising from business decline in individual areas. The Bank's operations also assists projects in which a number of member-states participate.

The European Investment Bank is an independent legal entity having its own agencies and financial resources. Its statutes establish the criteria to be used in examining investments. The Commission must express a view on each individual investment project intended for the Community. The Bank is also subject to guidance by the Commission, in that the latter indicates the preference to be given to regions, and the priorities to be observed within these regions. In a number of sectors associated with regional development the Bank will participate only when the Commission has established its policy.

In its investment policy the Bank naturally must act in accordance with the wishes of the member-states concerned. This obligation is embodied in one of its Articles.

Its first financial operations have been directed towards assisting the less developed regions of the Community. These still form the most important group in terms of the size of the credits advanced.

Financial assistance has also been made available to basic industries and electricity supply. At a later stage these activities have been extended to industry in general, as well as to agricultural products.

When the Commission eventually established priorities for the transport sector, the Bank also supported investments in this industry.

A start has been made also in considering decentralisation measures, as well as projects from small and medium-sized firms. Some of these financial projects cover several member-states. The first steps have been taken in financing industrial adjustments.

The funds available to the Bank naturally affect the extent and pace of its operations. To date these have not been limited through lack of funds; in this, the European Bank's experience corresponds to that of the World Bank. Resources consist of a paid-up capital of 250 million units (*i.e.* dollars at the current rate of exchange), and an authorised capital of 1,000 million units, borrowing powers as well as surpluses arising from its activity. These latter are credited to reserve. At present these funds amount to about 290 million dollars, of which about half is tied up in loans. To date, twenty loans have been granted to a total value of 154 million dollars. The average value of loans approximates to 7·7 million dollars, the sizes of loans ranging from 4,000 to 25 million dollars. This wide range reflects the great variety of the Bank's financial operations.

The total credits are apportioned approximately as follows:

about one-third goes to industry, a further third to transportation, a quarter to energy supply and the rest to agriculture.

The Bank's importance for regional policy is shown by a breakdown of loans according to country. Italy, whose needs are specifically mentioned in the Treaty, has received more than half of the total. France and the Federal Republic have each received about one-fifth, Belgium and Luxemburg about 3 per cent, while Holland so far has not made use of any credits.

The experience of the European Investment Bank corroborates the experience of similar international institutions specialising in making available credits for long periods: needs expand more rapidly than the extension of activity of such institutions.

An increase in the Bank's operations depends on a number of factors: prior agreement by governments, the continuously more detailed formulation of regional policy by the Community, together with increased investment activity by the public sector and by private firms on a regional basis.

The European Investment Bank believes that, to fulfil its tasks, it should extend its range of operations carefully and gradually.

The various tasks of the Bank will gradually expand since the Bank has only just started to make investments in certain fields of a regional character. This applies to major projects in new regions extending over national frontiers. As the Common Market more closely approaches its full realisation, these new regions may require investments to an extent which it is difficult to assess at present. The expanding tasks of the Bank will require fuller utilisation of its funds.

C. THE EUROPEAN SOCIAL FUND

The *European Social Fund* is a further means of assisting firms in meeting costs arising from adjustments to the Common Market. Regulation no. 9, which became operative on 20th September 1960, governs the Fund and establishes its legal basis (*Official Journal of the European Community*, 31st August 1960). The European Social Fund was established in conformity with *Articles 123* to *127* of the Rome Treaty. Its aims are: to improve employment opportunities of labour in the Community area, and to encourage the free movement and the better utilisation of labour. The European Social Fund, on the request of a member-state, meets half the costs incurred by a state or a public body for the following purposes:

(i) Re-employment of labour by means of retraining and resettlement.

(ii) Maintenance of the wages of employees whose work has been affected temporarily, or has ceased entirely, due to a firm's changing over to making other products.

1. RETRAINING AND TRANSFER TO OTHER LOCALITIES

Assistance by the Fund is for retraining with the object of making new employment opportunities accessible to the unemployed (if registered at a labour exchange).

Movement to other localities must involve movement within the Community with the object of obtaining new, productive and not seasonally limited employment. The change in place of residence must be officially arranged or agreed.

Changes in production by firms must be basic changes in production and must have as their object the manufacture of new products differing from existing products in other ways than by improvements or complementary additions to the existing product-range.

2. COST RECOVERIES

Support from the Fund is obtainable only after expenses have been incurred and the member-state must apply for assistance from the Fund. It is entirely up to the national government concerned to initiate claims on the Fund. Payments are made, not directly to the firms or employees concerned, but to the government for transmission to them.

The types of costs which may be recovered are:

> Operations of state institutions responsible for retraining and of public or private bodies under their direct control; subsistence, accommodation and travel allowances; incentive payments; costs of meeting claims for family assistance and social security; together with the wages, salaries and social security payments of the staff required for administration or teaching in the training institutions; and removal costs (*i.e.* travelling costs of the trainees, and immediate dependants; transport costs for removal of household goods, and other costs incurred by removal, including compensation to the family for separation).

To get a general idea of the types of organisation in the Community which may apply for help to the Social Fund, the following institutions in West Germany are listed in the *Official Journal of the European Community* (1st February 1962, pp. 145–62) as being eligible to apply for recovery of costs:

> *Berufsgenossenschaften* (professional and trade associations); *Bundesanstalt für Arbeitsvermittlung und Arbeitslosenversicherung* (Federal Ministry of Labour and Unemployment Insurance); *Bundesanstalt für den Güterverkehr* (Federal Department for Goods Transport); *Bundesbahnversicherungsanstalt* (Federal Railway Insurance Office); *Bundesversicherungsanstalt für Angestellte* (Federal Insurance Office for State Employees); *Feuerwehrkassen* (Firemen's Insurance Organisation); *Gemeinde-Unfallversicherungs-verbände* (Municipal Accident Insurance Associations); *Handwerkskammer* (Chambers of Craft Industries); *Industrie-und Handelskammer* (Chambers of Industry and Commerce); *Knappschaften* (Miners' Pension Insurance Societies); *Landesversicherungsanstalten* (Agricultural Insurance organisations); *Seekasse* (Maritime Benefit Fund).

VI Transactions by the Public Sector

Within the countries of the EEC, about one-third of total economic activity derives from the public sector. This percentage figure is admittedly an estimate, but there is no doubt that public expenditure plays an extremely important part in the economic life of all member-states of the Community.

A. THE EEC TREATY AND TRANSACTIONS BY THE PUBLIC SECTOR

No specific article in the Rome Treaty deals with transactions by the public sector. There is little doubt, however, that, as the spirit and content of the Treaty is being interpreted, the public sector in EEC countries is also being affected and consequently Europeanised. The most relevant is *Article 7* of the Treaty which states that, subject to certain exceptions, discrimination based on nationality is not permitted in EEC countries. It is generally accepted that discrimination is to be interpreted as any unjustified difference in treatment. Consequently, in placing public contracts, discrimination in member-states against other EEC nationals is not permitted.

Furthermore, *Article 90* of the Treaty, in dealing with employment in public corporations, public institutions and state monopolies, states that EEC member-countries within the framework of their public institutions may not take actions which do not accord with the regulations in *Article 7* forbidding discrimination.

Article 223 of the Treaty restricts the scope of these regulations by excluding from them the manufacture of weapons, ammunition and war material, and trade in these commodities. In consequence, the defence sector remains completely within national control and is in no way affected by the Treaty.

B. GERMAN ACTION

In April 1960 the Federal Ministry for Trade decreed that invitations to tender by public authorities would be equally open to home and foreign producers. It stated that the purchase of foreign products was desirable, both in view of Germany's satisfactory economic position and of the increasing degree of trade liberalisation, particularly inter-European business expansion. This action superseded the principle of reciprocity which had been acted on up to that date. This principle derived from a statement by the Federal Finance Ministry in May 1954 to the effect that foreign applicants would be considered only from those countries which were prepared to give equal consideration to German tenders.

The decree of April 1960 has loop-holes since it can be nullified if the economic position deteriorates and since it acknowledges a certain degree of protection for certain industries. The decree states that the purchasing authorities must be satisfied in regard to the expertise, ability and reliability of the foreign supplier. All relevant factors are to be taken into account in accepting the most favourable offer. Foreign suppliers must offer guarantees on fulfilment of contract, on supply of replacements and, in certain cases, on the care and maintenance of the installations supplied.

In spite of these limitations, however, the decree is a major step forward. In this field the Federal Republic is in the forefront of liberalisation.

C. POSSIBILITIES OF A EUROPEAN SOLUTION

Without doubt, discrimination against EEC nationals in other countries of the Community is contrary to the Treaty and any difference in treatment must be eliminated. The method of approach has been laid down in the EEC Treaty.

According to *Article 100 ff.* of the Treaty, the Council of Ministers may, on the advice of the Commission, establish guiding principles for adjusting those regulations of member-states which directly affect the structure or functioning of the Common Market.

Article 101 states further that the Commission should discuss with member-states the existing differences in administrative regulations. Should these discussions not succeed in eliminating distortions in competition, the Council may, during the current, second stage of transition by a qualified majority, issue "guiding principles" in line with the proposals of the Commission, so as to assist in harmonising the existing purchasing policies in EEC countries.

These principles must embrace the basic concepts which underlie the purchasing system in EEC countries. The first problem lies in devising a suitable method of inviting tenders. Public invitations to tender might be the safest approach from the point of view of eliminating discrimination. This principle need not be applied generally because in some sectors limited tenders have become accepted. Publication of invitations to tender would not of itself necessarily ensure abolition of discrimination by public authorities against other EEC nationals. Naturally, local firms or national firms are in a better position to be informed of public tenders than those in other countries. To take account fully of foreign suppliers, it has been suggested that invitations to tender should be published in all countries of the Community on a similar basis and simultaneously. The publication of an EEC "journal for tenders" is being considered. Probably the *Official Journal* itself will publish invitations to tender or will carry a special section in which tenders are publicised. The Treaty makes provision for the drawing up of a more effective regulation than the rather loose guiding principles set out in *Article 100*, and such a revised regulation is probable in view of the existing state of negotiations on this question.

D. EUROPEAN CONTROL

In the final instance, however, discrimination against foreign nationals in the Common Market can be obviated only if a supra-national organisation ensures observation of the regulations. Whether this organisation should be a court, an arbitration tribunal or merely a forum for discussion will be decided only after careful consideration of various political and other relevant factors. At all events, it is clear that a supra-national institution of some kind is required.

Liberalisation of the purchasing systems employed by public authorities is one of the most difficult problems raised by the Rome Treaty. Many divers interests—long established commercial and personal relationships—clash here with the principle of equality for all EEC Europeans. Progress, however, is assured even in this field, since the Commission in Brussels and the national governments are at work on these matters and some results have already been achieved. Confidence is further strengthened by the astonishingly quick consolidation of the Common Market after acceptance of the acceleration proposals in 1960 and the transition to the second period of development to fuller integration at the beginning of 1962.

Amongst the first results of inter-governmental discussions so far has been a synchronisation of regulations governing public authority purchasing, the right of domicile and free movement of services. In respect of public tenders involving constructional industries, it is intended that discrimination on grounds of domicile or discriminatory practices in service industries should be eliminated in member-states by 31st December 1963. Thus tenders from other EEC countries will be placed on an equal footing with home tenders from 1st January 1964. In practice, liberalisation should progress step by step as outlined in the proposals for the general program "of public purchases and service requirements" of 20th June 1961. These permit the following measure of protection for the national constructional industry:

If, in any one state, the volume of orders from public authorities, regional authorities and other public bodies undertaken by nationals or companies of other member states exceeds a certain quota, then the home state has the right to exclude individuals and companies from other countries from further orders until the end of the current year.

This quota is the same for all member-states and is a percentage figure of the average volume of public orders during the previous two years. The quota will increase every two years from 31st December 1963 to 31st December 1969.

Also relevant, although subject to exceptions, is the volume of public orders obtained by nationals or companies within the state from other member-states.

"Public orders", in the context of these regulations, are orders obtained directly from one state by nationals and companies of other member-states, such as:

Orders obtained directly by nationals and companies domiciled in other member countries.

Orders obtained by nationals or companies via subsidiaries or agencies in the state.

The EEC regulations will probably cover the following points:

(i) Public agencies of member-states, to be defined in more detail later, will probably be required from 1964 onwards to publicise invitations to tender for constructional work and tenders of high value in the proposed EEC "journal of tenders".

(ii) Lists of firms interested in public contracts will be established. All firms will be equally eligible to tender.

E. REGULATIONS IN INDIVIDUAL EEC COUNTRIES

Until complete liberalisation in purchases by public authorities has been established, *i.e.* until a journal for public tenders in the Community is launched, knowledge of existing regulations in individual EEC countries is essential.

1. In the *Federal Republic*, the legal basis for public purchases, other than civil construction, is the *Verdingungsordnung für Leistungen* (regulations governing fulfilment of public contracts), while civil construction is covered by *Verdingungsordnung für Bauleistungen* (regulations governing public contracts for building and construction). Public tenders are published in the *Öffentlichen Ausschreibungsblatt* (Public Tender Journal).

2. *Belgium* has a system similar to that of West Germany in regard to purchases by public authorities, and public tenders are the rule. The legal basis in Belgium is the regulations of 5th October 1955, published in the *Moniteur Officiel*, Brussels. Tenders are published in the *Bulletin des adjudications*.

3. In *France* a number of methods are used:

   (i) Public tenders.

   (ii) Limited tenders.

   (iii) Appel d'offres ouvert.

   (iv) Appel d'offres restreint.

   (v) Appel d'offres avec concours.

   (vi) Direct contact.

   (vii) At a price subject to change.

Of these various methods, only tenders would come within the scope of an EEC "Journal of tenders".

4. In *Italy* the legal basis is the *Royal Decree No. 2440* of 18th November 1923 (regulations governing the accountancy system of the state), together with the regulations enforcing this enactment published by the *Royal Decree No. 827* of 23rd May 1924. The following methods are used:

   (i) Public tenders.

   (ii) Limited tenders.

   (iii) Direct contact.

   (iv) Informal limited tenders.

Public tenders are published in the *Foglio Annunzi Legali* and in the official gazettes in the relevant provinces.

5. In *Luxemburg* the public purchasing system has its legal basis in the regulations of 29th December 1956. The following methods are used:

   (i) Public tenders.

   (ii) Limited tenders.

   (iii) Direct contact.

6. In the *Netherlands* the legal basis varies in different areas. However only two methods are in use—public and limited tenders. Public tenders are published either in the *Staatscourant* or in trade journals or in one or several newspapers.

PART IV

RETROSPECT AND PROSPECT

RETROSPECT AND PROSPECT

Four Years of the EEC

The Council of Ministers stated on 14th January 1962 that the objectives laid down in the Rome Treaty for the first period of transition had been substantially achieved. The fifth year of the EEC Community's existence began on 1st January 1962, the date which inaugurated the second period of transition. Thus the Community has made significant progress towards an economic union. Furthermore, from now on certain decisions of the Council of Ministers, although admittedly not the most important, no longer need to observe the unanimity rule as has hitherto been the case, but may be taken by qualified majority. These major achievements have encouraged the *Deutsche Industrie-und Handelstag* to review the first four years of the European economic union.

A. FULFILMENT OF THE TREATY

The Treaty's regulations regarding tariffs, duties and quotas, together with the acceleration decision of 12th May 1960, have been fulfilled. Since 1st January 1962 internal tariffs have been reduced by the following amounts from the level obtaining when the Treaty became operative: by 40 per cent for industrial products, by 35 per cent for non-liberalised agricultural products, and by 30 per cent for liberalised agricultural products. It is only in the Federal Republic that reductions in non-liberalised agricultural products have been limited to 30 per cent by the decision of the Bundestag and against the wishes of the government. The external tariffs were adjusted in all member-states towards a common external tariff. As a result, in the Federal Republic external tariffs on industrial products were slightly increased so that the second part of the 1957 reduction occasioned by boom conditions has been cancelled.

Article 4 of the acceleration decision required the elimination of all remaining quota restrictions on industrial products between member-states by 1st January 1962. All Community members, with the exception of Italy, carried out this decision. In line with *Article 7* of the acceleration decision of 12th May 1960, quotas in agricultural products, with some exceptions, were increased. Exceptions include, amongst others, the allotment of quotas for wine by the Federal Republic, Italy and France.

B. TREATY INFRINGEMENTS

Infringements of the regulations of the Treaty have been rare: all told, only about 20 cases have occurred in four years and these have not been very important. In some instances of failure by member-states to deal with contraventions of the Treaty, the Commission has not hesitated to call on the Court of the Community. Only three cases have been reported so far: two against Italy and one against the Federal Republic for its refusal to establish a global quota for certain types of meat and meat products in line with *Article 33* of the Treaty. One case has been decided against Italy; the other two are still pending.

C. TREATY AVOIDANCE

Of greater significance have been actions designed to get round the Treaty, *i.e.* actions which conflict, not with the wording, but with the spirit of the Treaty. For example, to mention a recent case, early in 1961 the Italian tobacco monopoly reduced prices for Italian cigarettes by approximately 15–20 per cent, while at the same time increasing turnover tax on imported and home-produced cigarettes. The result amounts in effect to discrimination against foreign cigarettes. Some measures of Treaty avoidance, for example tax discrimination on imported cars in Italy, have since been revoked.

On the whole the Community as a customs union has made satisfactory progress in spite of some blemishes. It has progressed even further than foreseen in the Treaty due to the acceleration decision of 12th May 1960.

It should be remembered, however, that the Community is not only a customs union; it is also intended to be a true economic union by the end of the transition period. The objects outlined in the Rome Treaty for the first transition period have to all practical purposes been achieved, not only with regard to tariffs, but also with regard to the first steps towards an economic union. A general programme has been accepted covering: the removal of limitations on right of domicile; the liberalisation of services; the freedom of movement of employees; the liberalisation of capital movements; regulations governing cartels; the first steps to the co-ordination of trade policy of member-states; and finally, after an almost dramatic struggle, agreement on the important elements of a common agricultural policy.

Not only have member-states and the institutions of the Community been active; industry itself has made an even more important contribution to the remarkable degree of consolidation of the Community during its first four years by increasing co-operation over national frontiers.

D. EXTERNAL RELATIONS OF THE EEC

The external relations of the Community changed suddenly and surprisingly in 1961. In many European states, governments and industries had been under the belief that a multilateral free trade area in various forms would be successful and would act as a bridge to the Community. The commercial difficulties arising sooner or later for non-members of the Community from the establishment of the EEC would thus be obviated or reduced. However, efforts in this direction up to 1961 were not successful. The only instance of success was the bilateral negotiation with Greece regarding her association with the Community. In contrast, the negotiations with Turkey were not so successful. At the beginning of 1961 it looked as if Europe might be divided into two economic blocs—EEC and EFTA.

Since then, however, the position has been radically altered by the decision of Britain, Denmark and Ireland to initiate negotiations with a view to joining the Community, and by the application of Sweden, Austria and Switzerland to establish a new basis for their relations with the Common Market. Outstanding new opportunities have been created. This development without doubt is due in the first instance to the firmness of the EEC Commission. The negotiations with Britain show, nevertheless, the difficulty of the problems requiring solution even with goodwill on all sides. German industry can only express the hope that these negotiations will soon be successful so that the danger of a gulf between the Community and EFTA is finally eliminated. At present EEC and EFTA are still separate. Should the problems arising from Britain's membership be solved, it will be easier to find solutions for other EFTA states.[1]

1. *Commenting on the Brussels break-down, Dr. Commer writes:*
The comments and conclusions of this book are in no way affected by the break-down in January 1963 of the negotiations on British membership of the EEC. Quite the contrary. Any move by Britain in the economic field to turn aside from the Continent would appear neither justified nor wise. Those who are engaged in business should seek all the more actively to participate in the European market as outlined in this book. It is encouraging to note that, since the end of the Brussels negotiations, British firms have undertaken investments in the EEC. At least one desirable result has emerged from these negotiations: *i.e.* some certainty of the position. Even had the negotiations not broken down, there would have been uncertainties since British membership could not have become an established fact much before 1965 due to such political factors as general elections in Britain, Italy and the Netherlands. It is to be hoped, however, that negotiations on tariffs within the framework of GATT will lead to a reduction in tariffs between EFTA and EEC countries.

Economic activity in the European market is now more essential than ever as this forms the basis of European integration. It will certainly withstand all political storms. In West Germany in particular the objective remains the same: Britain should become a member of an enlarged EEC in the not too distant future. And even the French president has declared that the United Kingdom will one day be a member of the European Community.

E. TRADE POLICY

A settlement of relations between the Community and EFTA will not, however, eliminate all difficulties arising from movement towards European unity. The question of trade relations with the countries of the Western world will become more urgent. The larger the European Common Market area, the greater will be its discriminatory effects in the long run on third countries, *i.e.* the United States, Central and South America, Japan and other Far Eastern countries. The proposals made to date for associating these states with the Community are extremely difficult because they imply a system of world-wide free trade of an extent which did not exist even prior to 1914. Moreover, such an extension of the EEC would completely destroy its political purpose. The function of the larger Community must therefore be to establish a liberal trade policy in relation to all states in the free world. Such a policy will be facilitated by the increasingly liberal tendency of the USA's own trade policy.

The fears frequently expressed that the creation of the EEC from its very inception would damage its world trading partners, and particularly its European trading partners, has fortunately not been confirmed in practice. Although trade within the Community area has increased to a greater extent than trade with other European countries and the world, its trade with the latter also has shown continuous increases. In any case, it is the purpose of a customs union—as well as of any free trade area—to facilitate trade of member-states with each other in relation to trade with third countries.

F. ECONOMIC EVALUATION

An economic evaluation depends on the criteria used. The results of the first four years are satisfactory when considered in relation to the minimum programme of the Rome Treaty regarding the first transition period. Treaty infringements and circumventions have not been very significant. How, then, have the advantages and disadvantages of the Treaty affected different member-states? France appears to have gained most, mainly because the Treaty enforced the liberalisation of French industry and an associated devaluation of the franc. Its gains, however, have benefited all partners.

The specific targets laid down in the Rome Treaty for the first transition period have been substantially achieved. The targets, however, were modest and success was greatly facilitated by the exceptionally favourable economic climate inside and outside the Community. Very little indeed has been achieved in matters not directly laid down in the Treaty, and the possibilities of increased integration of the economies of member-states have not been fully exploited. It has not been possible, for example, to establish a common trade policy in relation to state trading organisations in other countries or in relation to low wage-cost countries. An attempt by the Commission to limit the supply of crude oil from the Eastern bloc to the EEC broke down in July 1961 owing to the resistance of Italy, which obtains no less than 19 per cent of its crude oil requirements from that area. It is not enough for the Rome Treaty's provisions to be fulfilled just as if the Treaty were like any other treaty. Economic nationalism and protectionism have shown themselves remarkably tough in relation to the limited powers of the European authorities. Only the future can show whether or not the agreement on agriculture will turn out to be a triumph of collective protectionism of the Six with consequent disadvantages to the Community's relations with other trading partners and in particular with the countries under development. It must also be pointed out that the efforts of the European economies have not yet substantially affected the standard of living of broad sectors of the population.

The recall of Etienne Hirsch, the President of the Euratom Commission, who apparently had become too European for the French Government, shows how much *L'Europe des Patries* has become a reality. In spite of marked opposition to his recall from the European parliament and public opinion in the Community, and notwithstanding the more measured but nonetheless unequivocal regrets of France's partners in the Council of Ministers, Hirsch went and was replaced by a more nationalistic Frenchman of the Debré school. The lack of progress in amalgamating the three European communities (EEC, Euratom and the Coal and Steel Community) puts in question, unfortunately, the goodwill of some member governments. The difficulties experienced (for example, in rationalising the Belgian coal industry) by the Iron and Steel Community, in spite of its supra-national character and its ten years' existence, indicate that substantial progress has still to be made in industrial integration. It is certain, however, that economic nationalism in the six EEC countries has declined and that industry must adjust itself to continuing integration. The point of no return has been reached. There is no passage back to sovereign European national economies.

The following matters will be of particular importance to business firms during the second stage of the EEC Treaty, *i.e.* to 31st January 1965:

(i) Harmonisation of turnover taxes in EEC countries (new regulations with regard to turnover tax on products crossing frontiers).

(ii) Harmonisation of commercial laws in the Common Market (bankruptcy, executors, patents, trade marks and design).

(iii) A common transport policy.

(iv) The first executive regulations of EEC cartel policy (*Official Journal of the European Community*, 21st February 1962).

APPENDICES

I

Trade Movement within Europe

A. *Foreign trade of EEC countries with each other and with EFTA countries expressed as percentage of their total trade for the first half-year 1960 and first half-year 1961.*

	Imports				Exports			
	from the EEC		from EFTA		to the EEC		to EFTA	
	1960*	1961*	1960	1961	1960	1961	1960	1961
German Federal Republic ..	30	30	20	19	29	32	28	28
Belgium-Luxemburg	47	51	14	13	49	54	15	16
Netherlands ..	45	49	13	14	46	46	24	23
France	29	30	9	10	29	34	15	15
Italy	26	28	16	15	29	31	21	21

* First half-year only.

B. *Foreign trade of EFTA countries with each other and with EEC countries expressed as percentage of their total trade for the first half-year 1960 and first half-year 1961.*

	Imports				Exports			
	from the EEC		from EFTA		to the EEC		to EFTA	
	1960*	1961*	1960	1961	1960	1961	1960	1961
Denmark	39	40	36	38	29	28	42	43
Norway	31	32	39	40	25	25	42	44
Sweden	41	40	24	26	31	33	34	37
Switzerland ..	60	60	12	11	41	42	17	16
Austria	56	59	12	12	50	51	12	14
Great Britain ..	14	15	10	11	14	16	11	12
Portugal	38	34	20	25	21	21	19	23

* First half-year only.

II

Reduction of Customs Tariffs between the EEC Countries

A. DUTIES ON INDUSTRIAL PRODUCTS

from 1st January 1962:	60 per cent of the duty as at 1st January 1957.
from 30th June 1963[1]:	50 per cent of the duty as at 1st January 1957.
from 31st December 1964:	reduction by 10 per cent, *i.e.* to a level representing 40 per cent of the duty as at 1st January 1957.
from 31st December 1965:	reduction by 10 per cent to a level representing 30 per cent of the duty as at 1st January 1957.

The progress of further reductions in the third transitional period from 1st January 1966 to 31st December 1969 has been left open in the Treaty.

B. DUTIES ON AGRICULTURAL PRODUCTS

from 1st January 1962:	70 per cent of duty as at 1st January 1957.
from 30th June 1963[2]:	reduction by 10 per cent to a level representing 60 per cent of the duty as at 1st January 1957.
from 31st December 1964:	reduction by 10 per cent to a level representing 50 per cent of the duty as at 1st January 1957.
from 31st December 1965:	reduction by 10 per cent to a level representing 40 per cent of the duty as at 1st January 1957.

1. On 30th June 1962, as a result of the second "acceleration decision", internal tariffs were reduced by a further 10 per cent.

2. On 1st March 1962, tariffs on non-liberalised agricultural products were reduced by a further 5 per cent so that the tariff for these products now amounts to 65 per cent. From 30th June 1963, they will amount to 55 per cent; from 31st December 1964 to 45 per cent; and from 31st December 1965 to 35 per cent.

III

Harmonisation of External Duties—Common External Tariff

A. DUTIES ON INDUSTRIAL PRODUCTS

at 1st January 1962: First move towards harmonising external tariffs of member-states to the "final intended tariff": reduction of the difference between existing tariffs and the final tariff by 30 per cent. The final tariff is the original intended tariff less 20 per cent.

at 1st January 1966[1]: Second stage of harmonisation: reduction of differences between tariffs by a further 30 per cent.

at 1st January 1970: End of the third stage of harmonisation: full adoption of the Common Tariff by all EEC states.

B. DUTIES ON AGRICULTURAL PRODUCTS

at 1st January 1962: First stage in harmonising external tariffs of member states to the intended final EEC tariff: reduction of difference between tariffs by 30 per cent.

at 1st January 1966[1]: Second stage of harmonisation; reduction of difference between tariffs by a further 30 per cent.

at 1st January 1970: End of the third stage of harmonisation: full adoption of the Common Tariff by all EEC states.

1. It is expected that the second stage of harmonisation will take place at the same time as the reductions in inter-EEC tariffs to 40 per cent of the level obtaining at 1st January 1957. Due to the second "acceleration decision", this reduction to 40 per cent will be reached by 30th June 1963.

IV

European Development Fund
Review of the activities of the European Investment
Bank from 1959 to 1961

A. AS AT 1st JANUARY, 1962

221 proposals to a total value of 250 million monetary units*
    have been accepted
109 financial agreements to a total value of 215 million units
    have been signed covering 197 schemes
166 invitations to tender have been published
192 orders have been placed
  91 projects are being executed
   3 schemes have been completed

B. DIVISION ACCORDING TO SECTOR

Road construction	66,933,000 units*
Development of agricultural areas ..	59,316,000 units
Education	41,491,000 units
Health	36,277,000 units
Railways	22,197,000 units
Harbours	20,573,000 units
Housing and public utilities	15,343,000 units
Studies and research	9,428,000 units

271,558,000 units*

* 1 unit = 1 US dollar.

V

Credit Facilities in Western Germany

Apart from the European credit sources mentioned in the text, European Recovery Programme credits are available in Western Germany for medium-sized industrial firms for measures required to adjust to international competition. Arrangements have been made available for such credits in the ERP Economic Plan of 1961. Probably in the ERP Economic Plan of 1962 further capital for similar purposes will be made available. The firms request credit from their banks, who pass on the request to the Federal Fund for Reconstruction (*Kreditanstalt für Wiederaufban*). Only proposals which will lead to substantial changes in production programmes are considered. These credits are granted only provided "a substantial part of the existing means of production are replaced by new equipment". A request has to include the new production programme: this is compared in detail with the past output of the firm.

Credit requests are decided at the discretion of the Treasury and the Federal Ministry of Economics. One major criterion is whether the request originates in a production sector "which due to international competition is subject to substantial structural changes". A structural change caused by the Common Market is one caused by international competition and can therefore be dealt with on the basis of the above policy.

VI

Résumé of all Points Relevant to Business Activity in the European Market

A. GENERAL BUSINESS MEASURES

 1. Planning
 2. Organisation
 3. Advertising
 4. Public relations
 5. Market observation taking account particularly of area differences
 6. Market research
 7. Product design
 8. Price policy
 9. Establishing purchasing or sales subsidiaries
10. Establishing manufacturing subsidiaries
11. Establishing assembly plants
12. Recruiting employees
13. Trainee-exchanges
14. Co-operation in production with other firms
15. Inter-firm comparisons
16. Participation in trade fairs and exhibitions
17. Participation in EEC tenders

MEASURES SPECIFICALLY APPLICABLE TO PRODUCTION

1. Production planning
2. Capacity increase through increased planning
3. Changes in factory or production organisation
4. Rationalisation
5. Standardisation
6. Automation

B. SPECIAL TASKS OF FIRMS WITHIN THE FRAMEWORK OF THE EEC

1. Membership of and co-operation with Chambers of Industry and Commerce or trade associations.
2. Establishing associations for liaison with EEC authorities.
3. Encouraging employees to take part in lectures or seminars either as speakers or participants.

VII

Proposed Method of Export Market Analysis
(by permission of the Gesellschaft für Marktforschung, Hamburg)

An essential part of market analysis lies in interviews by experts and research workers working in the foreign country. These interviews must be carefully planned and properly directed. It is most important, therefore, to utilise fully the experience and "know-how" of experts in foreign countries and the knowledge of the employing firm in working out the questionnaires and scope of these interviews. This part of the work is referred to as *desk research*. The expertise consists in making use of the results of desk and *field research*.

The results should comprise:

    (a) a market assessment;
    (b) market sales prospects for the firm's products;
    (c) the type of sales effort required;
    (d) proposals for advertising and export agencies.

These results should be based on the table opposite:

Questions and Investigations in Market = Field Research

1. Desk research	2. Analysis of market demand	3. Analysis of competition	4. Analysis of retail outlets
1.1 General economic situation	2.1 Consumers and households	3.1 National competitors	4.1 Importers
1.2 Population and industrial statistics	2.2 Firms, converters, users, etc.	3.2 Foreign competitors	4.2 Wholesale trade
1.3 Production, import and export statistics	2.3 Public authorities	3.3 Sales programme	4.3 Retail trade
1.4 Consumer statistics	2.4 Persons and authorities influencing demand	3.4 Sales system and sales organisation	4.4 Buyers and consumer co-operatives
1.5 Addresses and trade literature	2.5 Purchasing power	3.5 Price, condition and delivery time	4.5 Salesmen and agents
1.6 Trade associations and public authorities	2.6 Purchasing and consumer habits	3.6 Reputation and market position	4.6 Trade usage
1.7 Press, radio and sales agents	2.7 Arguments and assumptions (market climate)	3.7 Sales centre of gravity according to demand and regions	4.7 Trade margins and commissions
1.8 Import regulations	2.8 Attitude to quality, price, trade mark, form, colour, etc.	3.8 Service for and to customers	4.8 Price position and range
1.9 Customs tariffs and other duties	2.9 Assessment of the employing firm's product	3.9 Advertising	4.9 Influence of public authorities

VIII

Facilities for European Business Training in Western Germany

The *C. Rudolf Poensgen Institute* has been referred to in the main text (p. 72). The study courses of this institute are divided into a preliminary course and two main courses, each of two weeks' duration with an interlude of about five to six weeks during which members return to their firms. For 1962 and 1963, five courses have been proposed. Further details may be obtained from the Institute, Düsseldorf, Berliner Allee 10. In South Germany the Bavarian Economic School (München 13, Tengstrasse 37) is relevant.

The following organisations have also performed useful work in this field: the *Deutsche Gesellschaft für Betriebswirtschaft*, Berlin; the *Rationalisierungskuratorium der Deutschen Wirtschaft*, Frankfort-on-Main, with its provincial groups; the *Juniorenkreise der Deutschen Unternehmerschaft*; and the *Jungen Unternehmer der Arbeitsgemeinschaft Selbständiger Unternehmer*. Important basic problems of "European leadership" are discussed within the framework of science and economics.

The *Europa-Union Deutschland*, founded to provide information on European questions (General Secretariat: Stockenstr. 1–5, Bonn), and containing 11 provincial associations and 300 district and local associations), deals with questions of European economic policy. It holds an average of 180 meetings each month. A good example of the special information *Europa-Union Deutschland* makes available to leading industrialists is the meeting held in Essen in December 1961 on the subject: "Energy in Greater Europe". Five hundred leading experts from the power industry took part. Similar special meetings were held in 1962 on the following subjects: "Harmonisation of taxation systems in the Common Market"; "Problems of competition within the European economic community"; "European transport problems with special reference to marine transportation"; and "Agriculture in the Common Market".

The *Bildungswerk Europäische Politik* (Unter Sachsenhausen 6, Cologne) specialises in business management, and organises "briefing" sessions, seminars, study conferences and study tours lasting from 3 to 14 days. Through lectures, discussions, study tours and visits to European organisations, an attempt is made, generally with remarkable success, to acquaint participants with the general background as well as with the detailed subject matter. People of similar interests are invited to these meetings, *i.e.* people having the same profession. Such groups are, for example, leaders and potential leaders in industry, administration, publicity and agriculture. These meetings take place in the country in the following *Europa-houses*:

Europa-Haus Schliersee e. V., Neuhaus am Schliersee/Obb.

Europa-Haus Otzenhausen, Otzenhausen/Saar.

Haus Lerbach, Lerbach bei Bergisch-Gladbach, near Cologne.

Examples of some of the subjects covered in these seminars are: "Competition in EEC countries"; "Taxation in the Common Market"; "External trade policy of the Common Market"; and "Co-operation with associated countries".

Firms should establish contact with the above-mentioned organisations and the *Europa-Houses*, obtain information on programmes and send their employees to these seminars.

In addition the following deserve special mention as being active in European training: the *Friedrich-Ebert-Stiftung e. V.*, Koblenzer Strasse 54, Bonn; and the *Heimvolkshochschule*, Bergneustadt, Rhineland.

IX

Books in English on the Common Market

Much of the material in this Appendix is based on a survey of British publications on the subject of the Common Market in *The Times Review of Industry,* December 1962. It appears here in a modified form by kind permission of the Editor of the Review.

A. PUBLICATIONS OF THE EUROPEAN COMMUNITIES

(Obtainable from the Information Service of the European Communities: 23 Chesham Street, London, S.W.1, or Suite 808 The Farragut Building, Washington 6, D.C.)

> *The Facts* (1s.)
> *The Six in Figures* (1s.)
> *The Common Market* (1s.)

These booklets, with occasional brochures like: *Euratom* (2s.); *Community Topics* (2s.); *The ECSC* (free); *The Development Fund* (free) and the Information Service's monthly *Bulletin,* provide useful basic information for the general reader. They are, in the main, general pamphlets concerned either with the broad details or with particular aspects of the Communities.

More detailed, legal and official information—the *Official Journal of the European Communities,* texts of the Treaties and the large number of technical reports—can be obtained through Her Majesty's Stationery Office, and in the United States from the Superintendent of Documents, Government Printing Office.

B. SPECIAL STUDIES

1. *Britain and Europe:* Economist Intelligence Unit, 16s.

Published in 1957, this is a pioneer handbook in the field of European Economic co-operation. It represents the first detailed survey of what free trade in Europe is likely to mean for British industry, and is a comprehensive report on a vast and objective research project carried out by the Economist Intelligence Unit in Britain and on the Continent. The facts on which the Unit's conclusions are based are given in full. As well as discussing the impact of free trade, both in its EEC and EFTA forms, on major industrial sectors, the book contains a statistical appendix on trade between members of EEC and EFTA by major classes of manufacture.

2. *Commonwealth and Europe:* Economist Intelligence Unit, 42*s*.

3. *The Common Market*, by J. F. Deniau: Barrie & Rockliff with Pall Mall Press, 18s. Published in the United States by Frederick A. Praeger, $5.00.

Now in its third edition, this work is by now a classic on the subject. The author, one of the Commission's younger leading civil servants, makes what is an extremely complex subject appear simple and relates the various strands to each other.

4. *The Challenge of the Common Market*, by U. W. Kitzinger: Blackwell, 10s. 6d. A completely revised edition, under the title of *The Politics of Atlantic Integration*, is published in the United States by Frederick A. Praeger, $5.50.

In this book, now in its fourth edition, Dr. Kitzinger, of New College, Oxford, is not concerned solely with the structure of the Common Market, but examines also why the Common Market came about, what it is, what has happened to it since its inception, and what British membership would mean—to Britain, the Commonwealth and Europe. The author supports British entry and argues the case against opponents of it, producing a useful book for the politically minded.

5. *The Community of Europe*, by Richard Mayne: Gollancz, 21*s*. Published in the United States by Norton, $4.00.

A Cambridge historian by training, the author is a Press Officer at Brussels. This well-written book can be read for pleasure as well as for information. It examines the historical background of the movement to integration in Europe and explains what people mean by "Europe" and what the politicians are talking about when they speak of European unity. The book contains copious notes and includes an excellent bibliography.

6. *The Political Future of the European Community*, by Roy Pryce: Marshbank and Federal Trust, 15*s*.

Like Mr. Mayne, Dr. Pryce is a former Cambridge don now working for the Commission (he is in charge of the Community's Information Service in London). His book deals with the difficult problems of the future structure and character of the European Community. It is a good guide to issues which are going to be of paramount importance in coming years, and details much of the European thinking on political union, particularly on the limits of what is possible.

7. *Britain and the Common Market*, by John Pinder: Cresset Press, 12*s*. 6*d*.

Mr. Pinder, Director of International Operations at the Economist Intelligence Unit, outlines the context of the debate on Britain's entry—the balance of political forces in the Community, with de Gaulle's concept of a Grand Alliance in contradistinction to the concept of full integration, the motives leading to the establishment of the Common Market and the provisions of the Rome Treaty. The arguments of special British interests are examined, as are the positions of Commonwealth exporters and EFTA countries, and set in balance with the political issue of whether or not Britain should take a direct part in reshaping Europe. Although the author makes it clear that he supports full British participation in the Community, his book provides a useful, reasoned assessment of both sides of the case.

8. *A Short Guide to Market Research in Europe*, by Max K. Adler: Crosby, Lockwood and Son, 15*s*.

This is so far the only introductory work in English on this subject. Its usefulness to market research men is limited, since it treats of matters they presumably know of already. But it may be useful to their customers in that it serves to remind them that, although the Common Market is being created, it is not yet really in being.

9. Other special studies are:

> *The Common Market Today—and Tomorrow*, by Michael Shanks and John Lambert: Chatto and Windus, 25*s*. Published in the United States by Frederick A. Praeger, $6.95.

Europe at Sixes and Sevens, by Emile Benoit: Columbia University Press, $6.00 (paperback $1.95).

The European Common Market: an Analysis of Commercial Policy, by Isaiah Frank: Frederick A. Praeger, $7.50. Published in Britain by Stevens and Sons, 55s.

The United States and the Common Market: A Background Study, by Don D. Humphreys: Frederick A. Praeger, $4.50.

Western Unity and the Common Market, by Walter Lippmann: Brown, $2.75.

American Enterprise in the European Common Market, edited by Eric Stein and Thomas L. Nicholson (2 vols.): University of Michigan Press, $30.00.

U.S. Trade and the Common Market, by William L. Clayton: New York, Foreign Policy Association.

C. STUDY PUBLICATIONS AND PERIODICALS

1. *Britain in Europe:* Bow Group, Conservative Political Centre, 2s. 6d.

This list does not cover the many political pamphlets published on Common Market issues, but an exception is made in respect of this Bow Group publication because it contains, at the end, a valuable analysis of who takes what decisions and of the voting mechanism of decision-making in the Community, together with a good short summary of the Rome Treaty's provisions and how these may affect Britain.

2. Political and Economic Planning (PEP) series: available from George Allen and Unwin.

   Trade Unions and the Common Market, 4s.
   Cartel Policy and the Common Market, 7s. 6d.
   Negotiations on Political Union, 3s. 6d.
   Atlantic Tariffs and Trade, 4s.
   Proposals for a Common Agricultural Policy, 3s. 6d.
   Food Prices and the Common Market, 2s. 6d.
   Agriculture, the Commonwealth and EEC, 6s.

PEP has also published *Aspects of European Integration*, an Anglo-French symposium (15*s*.).

3. Economist Intelligence Unit: dossiers and periodicals:

> *If Britain Joins*, 6*s*.
> *Taxes for Britain: Impact of Common Market*, 6*s*.
> *Six-monthly Supplement on EEC*, £5 per annum
> *Quarterly Economic Reviews of EEC Countries*, £42 per annum
> *Quarterly Economic Reviews of all Western European Countries*, £145 per annum
> *Marketing in Europe:* published monthly, annual subscription £30

4. *Journal of Common Market Studies*, edited by Uwe Kitzinger: Blackwell, three issues yearly: annual subscription 30*s*.

A regular commentary on developments in Europe, particularly useful to industrialists.

5. *The European Common Market:* a bibliography with commentary, by J. E. Wild: The Library Association, 9*s*.

This includes a general introduction to the subject, lists books, pamphlets, reports and articles and contains both author and subject indices. Now in its third edition, this is probably the most up-to-date bibliography in English.

6. HMSO publications:

> *The Rome Treaty:* text of treaty, 10*s*.
> *Britain and the European Community*, 3*s*.

7. American publications on the Common Market of this kind.

Virtually complete bibliographies of the enormous range of material available in the United States on the Common Market can be obtained in America from the Superintendent of Documents, Government Printing Office (or through the regional offices of the U.S. Department of Commerce), and from the European Community Information Service in Washington.

Many periodicals, including *International Organisation* (published by the World Peace Foundation in Boston), *International Commerce* (a Department of Commerce publication), *The American Economic Review* and *Current Economic Indicators* (published at the United

Nations), contain articles and studies on the Common Market. The university law reviews and political science quarterlies, of which there are many all over the country, are also a good source for such material. The Foreign Policy Association, the National Industrial Conference Board, the centres for international studies in all the major public and private universities, and the larger banks (particularly the Chase Manhattan Bank), also provide much varied analytical and statistical information, as does the Department of Commerce. The Chamber of Commerce and the U.S. Council of the International Chamber of Commerce also issue brochures and guides to Common Market affairs.

X

Principal European Associations of Industry and Trade

(The addresses of organisations given below derive in part from a publication of the EEC Commission and are correct as at 1st January 1961)

GENERAL INDUSTRIAL AND TRADING ORGANISATIONS

Union of Industries of the EEC (UNICE):
4, rue Ravenstein, BRUSSELS: *tel. 13.45.62*

Standing Conference of Chambers of Commerce of the EEC:
c/o Kamer van Koophandel en Fabrikien voor Rotterdam Beursgebour, Coolsingel 58, ROTTERDAM

Committee of Trading Associations in EEC Countries:
31, Avenue Pierre Ier-de-Serbie, PARIS 16: *tel. KLÉber 67.30; 68.50*

European Working Group of International Trade Fair Associations:
7, Avenue George V, PARIS 8; *tel. BALzac 08.93*

EEC Committee of the International Bureau of Wholesalers:
48, Avenue de Villiers, PARIS 17: *tel. CARnot 65.24*

EEC Section of the International Association of Large Sales Organisations:
3, rue de la Science, BRUSSELS: *tel. 13.38. 20*

EEC Association of National Consumer Co-operative Organisations:
17, Place Emile Van der Velde, BRUSSELS: *tel. 13.28.60*

BUILDING INDUSTRY AND ANCILLARIES

1. General Organisations

Standing Committee for Examining Common Market Problems in the Construction and Building Industries:
3, rue de Berri, PARIS 8: *tel. ELYsée 48.25; 47.65*

Union of National Associations of Traders in Building Materials in the EEC:
3, Passage des Postes, BRUSSELS: *tel. 17.97.25; 18.09.75*

2. Bricks, Tiles and Accessories

European Association of Building Accessories Manufacturers:
2, Avenue Hoche, PARIS 8: *tel. CARnot 00.90*

Common Market Committee of Brick and Tile Manufacturers:
2, Avenue Hoche, PARIS 8: *tel. CARnot 34.15*

Association of EEC Ceramic Tile Manufacturers:
60, rue Ravenstein, BRUSSELS: *tel. 11.55.44; 13.02.94*

Working Group for EEC Problems of the Association of Sanitary Ceramics Manufacturers:
Via Filippo Corridoni 3, MILAN: *tel. 792.722*

Standing Conference of the European Enamel Product Industries (EUREMAIL):
Hochstrasse 115, HAGEN (West Germany)

Standing Committee of EEC Glass Industries:
3, rue La Boétie, PARIS 8: *tel. ANJou 46.47; 60.02*

3. Paints and Decorating Materials

Study Group of EEC Painters and Calendars:
1, Place de la Calandre, GHENT: *tel. 25.72.03*

Liaison Office of the EEC Paint, Lacquer and Printing Ink Manufacturing Associations:
42, Avenue Marceau, PARIS 8: *BALzac 63.70*

EEC Executive Committee of the European Association of Brush and Paint Brush Industries:
36, Avenue Hoche, PARIS 8: *tel. CARnot 00.90*

4. Timber

Central Organisation of EEC Timber Trades:
Galerie du Centre, BRUSSELS: *tel. 11.95.37; 11.98.77*

Executive Committee of EEC Timber Industries:
36, Avenue Hoche, PARIS 8: *tel. CARnot 00.90*

Association of the Tropical Timber Trade in the EEC:
Galerie du Centre, BRUSSELS: *tel. 11.95.37; 11.98.77*

Association of the Coniferous Timber Trade in the EEC:
Galerie du Centre, BRUSSELS: *tel. 11.95.37; 11.98.77*

European Federation of Pit Props Associations:
Secretariat: 27, rue N. Bosret, NAMUR (Belgium): *tel. 253.62*

Union of EEC Saw Mills Associations:
Galerie du Centre, Bloc 2, BRUSSELS: *tel. 11.95.37; 11.98.77*

CHEMICAL MATERIALS AND PRODUCTS INDUSTRIES

International Secretariat of the EEC Chemical Industries Association:
32, rue Joseph II, BRUSSELS: *tel. 18.44.40*

Liaison Committee of EEC Plastics Processing Industries:
3, rue Copernic, PARIS 16

Association of Trade Fertilisers in the EEC:
Piazza G. G. Belli 2, ROME

FOOD AND DRINK TRADES

A. FOOD

1. General Trading

International Union of Food Importers and Wholesalers Associations, EEC Committee of:
8, rue de L'Arsenal, LUXEMBURG: *tel. 5.28.51*

2. Dairy Produce

European Association of Dairy Trades:
Münsterstrasse 9, BONN: *tel. 3.73.54*

Dairy Industry Association of the EEC:
140, Boulevard Haussmann, PARIS 8: *tel. CARnot 12–51*

European Association of Trade in Milk and Milk Products—Wholesale, Imports, Exports:
4, rue de la Lingerie, PARIS: *tel. GUTenberg 10–65*

European Union of Wholesalers in Eggs, Egg Products and Poultry:
Utrechtsweg 266, DE BILT (Netherlands): *tel. Utrecht 6.01.41*

EEC Association of Canned Milk Producers:
140, Boulevard Hausmann, PARIS 8: *tel. MACmahon 40–63*

3. Edible Oils

Association of EEC Traders in Oil and Animal Fats and Derivatives:
Westersingel 43, ROTTERDAM

EEC Association of the Edible Oil Industries:
121, rue Royale, BRUSSELS: *tel. 17.26.14*

EEC Association of the Margarine Industries:
55, rue de la Loi, BRUSSELS: *tel. 12.05.26; 12.15.20; 12.57.74*

4. Grains

Central Organisation of EEC Millers:
(i) 66, rue de la Boétie, PARIS 8: *tel. ELYsée 45–60*
(ii) 165, rue du Midi, BRUSSELS: *tel. 12.17.78*

Committee of the Grain Trade in the EEC:
Posthoornstraat 13a, ROTTERDAM: *tel. 13.92.70*

Maize Converters, EEC Association of:
149, Bourse de Commerce, rue de Viarmes, PARIS I: *tel. CENtral 30–43*

Rice Starch Industries, EEC Liaison Committee of:
3, Allée Verte, BRUSSELS

Seed Corn Committee of the EEC:
24, rue des Fripiers, BRUSSELS: *tel. 17.79.94*

Wheat Starch Industries, EEC Secretariat of:
Marienstrasse 32, BONN: *tel. 3.77.30*

5. Fish

Association of the EEC Fish Industries:
55, rue de la Loi, BRUSSELS: *tel. 12.15.20; 12.05.26; 12.57.74*

6. Fruit and Vegetables

Association of Fruit Wholesalers in EEC Countries:
Von-Groote-Strasse 7, Marienburg, COLOGNE: *tel. 38.57.51*

EEC Central Union of the Associations of the Potato Starch Industries:
Hoofdstraat 82, HOOGEZAND (Netherlands): *tel. 05900; 2244*

Committee of the Potato Trade in EEC Countries:
220, Bourse de Commerce, rue de Viarmes, PARIS I: *tel. GUTenberg 57–49*

European Organisation for the Vegetable Preserving Industries:
38, Boulevard du Régent, BRUSSELS: *tel. 12.79.35; 12.79.42; 12.79.44*

Association of Industries Preserving Fruit and Vegetables in Vinegar, Salt, and Oil, and of Related Products:
Breestraat 81, LEYDEN: *tel. 22644; 22645*

7. Meat and Meat Products

European Association of Meat Wholesalers:
59, rue Saint-Lazare, PARIS 9: *tel. TRInité 91–33; 05–69; 50–92*

Cattle Trade Association, EEC Committee of:
29, rue Fortuny, PARIS 7: *tel. MACmahon 11–05*

Meat Processing Industries, EEC Liaison Committee of:
7, rue Alfred-de-Vigny, PARIS: *tel. CARnot 22–26; WAGram 85–84; 85–85*

EEC Committee of Slaughterhouse Organisations:
36, rue de l'Industrie, BRUSSELS: *tel. 12.47.77*

European Association of Fodder Manufacturers:
27, rue des Paroissiens, BRUSSELS: *tel. 12.09.55*

8. Prepared Foods and Condiments

EEC Association of Dietary Food Manufacturers:
23, rue Notre-Dame-des-Victoires, PARIS 2: *tel. GUTenberg 43–95*

European Committee of Soup Making Associations:
Bourse de Commerce, rue de Viarmes, PARIS I; *tel. GUTenberg 24–39*

EEC Board of the Mustard Industries:
55, rue de la Loi, BRUSSELS: *tel. 12.15.20; 12.05.26; 12.57.74*

Permanent Board of EEC Vinegar Industries:
23, rue Notre-Dame-des-Victoires, PARIS 2: *tel. CENtral 44–41*

9. Sugar Producers and Users, Confectionery and Pastry

Association of the Sugar Trade in the EEC
38, Boulevard du Régent, BRUSSELS: *tel. 12.79.42*

Association of European Sugar Producers:
23, Avenue d'Iéna, PARIS 16: *tel. KLÉber 62–86*

EEC Liaison Committee of Glucose Manufacturers:
Kneuterdijk 8, THE HAGUE: *tel. 183080*

EEC Association of the Confectionery Industries (CAOBISCO):
65, rue de la Loi, BRUSSELS: *tel. 12.05.20; 12.57.74*

European Organisation of the Jam and Fruit Preserving Industries:
55, rue de la Loi, BRUSSELS: *tel. 12.05.20; 12.57.74*

EEC Union of the Pastry Makers Association:
28, rue du Fossé-aux-Loups, BRUSSELS: *tel. 17.56.86*

EEC Union of National Associations of Bakeries and Baked Confectionery Trades:
147, rue Delaunoy, BRUSSELS: *tel. 27.27.72*

EEC Association of Confectioners:
38, rue des Pierres, BRUSSELS: *tel. 11.11.55*

EEC Committee of Yeast Manufacturers:
7, rue Léonce Reynaud, PARIS 16: *tel. PASsy 33–82*

B. DRINK

1. Alcoholic

EEC Committee for Traders in and Producers of Wine, Aromatic Wine, Sparkling Wine and Dessert Wine:
49, rue de Trèves, BRUSSELS: *tel. 11.38.05*

European Alcohol, Brandy and Spirit Association:
38, Boulevard du Régent, BRUSSELS: *tel. 12.79.42*

EEC Working Union of Brewery Associations:
Herengracht 282, AMSTERDAM: *tel. 6.26.46*

EEC Working Committee of Malting Houses:
85, Boulevard Emile-Jacqumain, BRUSSELS: *tel. 17.13.99*

Committee of the Hop Trade in the EEC:
27, rue de la Limite, BRUSSELS: *tel. 17.09.90*

European Union of Beer Wholesale Trade Association:
88a, Chaussée de Charleroi, BRUSSELS: *tel. 38.23.25*

2. Non-alcoholic

European Tea Committee:
86, Avenue Paul Deschanel, BRUSSELS: *tel. 15.50.60*

EEC Association of Manufacturers of Coffee Extract in Powder Form:
55, rue de la Loi, BRUSSELS: *tel. 12.15.20*

EEC Committee of the International Association of Unfermented Fruit Juice Manufacturers:
16, Chaussée d'Antin, PARIS 9: *tel. PROvence 70.22; 09.59; 66.43*

EEC Committee of the Food and Vegetable Juice Industries:
16, Chaussée d'Antin, PARIS 9: *tel. PROvence 70.22; 09.69; 66.43*

European Association of Natural Mineral Water Sales Organisations (UNESEM)
53, Boulevard Haussmann, PARIS 9: *tel. OPEra 37.33*

Union of the Associations of Carbonated Drink Manufacturers (UNESDA):
47, rue Hayvaert, BRUSSELS: *tel. 21.01.90*

FUEL AND POWER INDUSTRIES AND TRADES

Study Group of West European Coal Producers:
31, Avenue des Arts, BRUSSELS: *tel. 13.28.10*

EEC Committee of the International Union of Electricity Producers and Distributors:
12, Place des Etats-Unis, PARIS 16: *tel. LABorde 90.00*

International Association of Private Industrial Producers of Electricity (FIPACE):
18–24, rue des Colonies, BRUSSELS: *tel. 12.23.42*

European Association of Tallow Makers:
174, Avenue Victor-Hugo, PARIS 16: *tel. PASsy 23.41*

European Liaison Committee of Fuel Traders and Purchasers (CELNUCO):
62, Boulevard Flandrin, PARIS 16

HEAVY METAL INDUSTRIES

Commission for European Institutions of the Committee of European Foundry Industry Associations:
2, rue de Bassano, PARIS: *tel. KLÉber 81.02*

Executive Committee of the Non-Ferrous Scrap Trade in EEC Countries:
4, Boulevard Anspach, BRUSSELS: *tel. 17.99.92/93*

Liaison Committee of EEC Non-Ferrous Metal Industries (Foundries, Rolling Mills, Wire Manufacturers, Mines):
30, Avenue de Messine, PARIS 8: *tel. LABorde 87.56*

LIGHT METAL AND MACHINERY INDUSTRIES

Liaison Committee of the European Machinery Construction and Metal Using Industries:
15, rue Beaujon, PARIS 8: *tel. CARnot 32.77*

European Secretariat of Light Metal Packaging Manufacturers:
21, rue des Drapiers, BRUSSELS: *tel. 11.23.70*

EEC Committee of the International Liaison Office of Agricultural Machinery Traders and Repairers:
Stadhouderslaan 126, THE HAGUE: *tel. 51.23.11*

Committee of EEC Manufacturers of Refrigeration Engineering Products:
>   10, Avenue Hoche, PARIS 8: *tel. MACmahon 38.00*

European Committee of Dry Cleaning and Commercial Laundry Equipment Manufacturers:
>   11, Avenue Hoche, PARIS 8: *tel. MACmahon 38.00*

Association of EEC Sewing Machine Manufacturers (ASCOMAGE):
>   Via Brisa 3, MILAN: *tel. 87.24.23*

European Committee of Weighing Machine Manufacturers:
>   36, Avenue Hoche, PARIS 8: *tel. MACmahon 38.00*

European Committee of Armature Industries:
>   21, rue des Drapiers, BRUSSELS: *tel. 11.23.70*

PAPER TRADES

International Association of the Paper and Cardboard Wholesale Trade in the EEC:
>   76, Avenue Marceau, PARIS 9: *tel. ELYsée 43.35*

EEC Committee of the European Association of Corrugated Cardboard Manufacturers:
>   36, rue de Châteaudun, PARIS 9: *tel. TRInité 53.77; 53.78*

PHARMACEUTICAL PRODUCTS

International Association of Pharmaceutical Industries:
>   32, rue Joseph II, BRUSSELS: *tel. 18.44.40*

EEC Pharmacists' Association:
>   11, rue Archimède, BRUSSELS: *tel. 33.98.20*

International Association for Trade in Pharmaceutical Products in the EEC:
>   6, rue da la Trémouille, PARIS 8: *tel. BALzac 12.37*

PRECISION AND CRAFT TRADES

Committee of the Craft Associations of EEC Countries:
>   14, rue Duquesnoy, BRUSSELS: *tel. 11.91.58*

International Association of EEC Retail Trades in Clocks, Watches, Jewellery and Gold Articles:
>   52, rue D'Artois, BRUSSELS: *tel. 11.67.20*

European Committee of the Precision and Optics Industries:
Habsburgerring 2–12, COLOGNE: *tel. 21.44.58*

EEC Association of Opticians:
10, Avenue Groelstveld, BRUSSELS: *tel. 12.75.26; 13.24.88*

EEC Working Group of the European Association of Porcelain and Pottery Manufacturers (Tableware and Jewellery):
60, rue Ravenstein, BRUSSELS: *tel. 11.55.44; 13.02.94*

RUBBER AND LEATHER MATERIALS AND PRODUCTS INDUSTRIES

Liaison Office of the EEC Rubber Industries:
19, Avenue des Arts, BRUSSELS: *tel. 18.49.40*

Advisory Office of the EEC Committee of the Raw Hides Industry:
2, rue Edouard-VII, PARIS 9: *tel. OPEra 68.60*

Study Group of EEC Tanners Associations:
122, rue de Provence, PARIS: *tel. LABorde 96.45*

Common Market Liaison and Study Committee of the Footwear Industry:
2, rue Edouard-VII, PARIS: *tel. OPEra 68.60*

European Central Organisation of Boot and Shoe Wholesalers:
34, rue Dr. de Reuse, Mont St. Aman, GHENT: *tel. 28.10.18/19*

TEXTILE, CLOTHING AND FURNISHING FABRIC INDUSTRIES

1. General Trading Organisations

Common Market Committee of the European Union of National Associations of Textile Retailers (AEDT):
18, rue des Bons Enfants, PARIS 1: *tel. CENtral 24.70; 98.14*

EEC Working Group of the International Union of Textile Purchasers Associations (IVT):
Neumarkt 14, COLOGNE: *tel. 21.44.56/67*

2. Cotton and Wool Manufacturing

Committee of the Cotton Industries of the EEC:
1, Place de la Calandre, GHENT: *tel. 09.25.35.97; 09.23.19.01*

Liaison Organisation of the EEC Wool Industries:
24, rue Montoyer, BRUSSELS: *tel. 13.19.50*

Common Market Committee of the Sewing Yarn Industries:
37, rue de Courcelles, PARIS 8: *tel. MACmahon 06.11*

3. *Other Natural Fibre Industries*

Common Market Committee of the International Flax and Hemp Association:
37, rue de Courcelles, PARIS 8: *tel. MACmahon 06.11*

EEC Working Group of the European Jute Industries Associations:
33, rue Miromesnil, PARIS 8: *tel. ANJou 28.05*

EEC Working Group of the Union of European Coconut Fibre Industries:
Keizersgracht 230, AMSTERDAM: *tel. 22.18.22*

4. *Synthetic Fibre Industries*

EEC Working Group of the International Association of Chemical Fibre Yarn Processors:
24, rue Montoyer, BRUSSELS: *tel. 13.19.50*

EEC Group of the International Committee for Rayon and Synthetic Fibres:
(i) 29–31, rue de Courcelles, PARIS 8: *tel. BALzac 87.10*
(ii) 4, Chaussée de Charleroi, BRUSSELS: *tel. 37.12.20*

5. *Clothing, Fabrics and Carpets*

Inter-Trade Committee of the EEC Clothing Industry:
20, Avenue des Arts, BRUSSELS: *tel. 11.59.80; 11.59.89*

Secretariat of EEC Knitwear Industries:
24, rue Montoyer, BRUSSELS: *tel. 13.19.50*

European Bedding Union:
Königsallee 68, DUSSELDORF

European Association of Narrow Woven, Plaited and Elastic Fabrics:
Eusebiusbuitensingel 5, ARNHEM: *tel. 33447*

International Committee of Carpet and Furniture Fabric Manufacturers (CITTA):
Alexanderstrasse 18, Elberfeld, WUPPERTAL: *tel. 41251/52*

6. *Ancillary Industries*

EEC Study Group of the Textile Equipment Industries:
1, Place de la Calandre, GHENT: *tel. 25.72.03 (09)*

Working Group of EEC Textile Printers:
Kronprinzenstrasse 39, BONN: *tel. 5.14.95*

VEHICLE EQUIPMENT INDUSTRY

Liaison Committee for Components and Replacements (Vehicles):
Westendstrasse 61, FRANKFURT-ON-MAIN: *tel. 77.13.47*

Liaison Committee for Trailers and Surface Mounting Equipment Industries:
Westendstrasse 61, FRANKFORT-ON-MAIN: *tel. 77.13.47*

Common Market Committee for Bicycle Accessories and Replacement Parts:
21, rue des Drapiers, BRUSSELS: *tel. 11.23.70*

MISCELLANEOUS

EEC Sub-Committee of the International Trade in Flowers and Decorative Plants:
Kenaupark 31, HAARLEM: *tel. 1.19.88*

International Association of Flower Wholesalers:
Stadhoudersplantsoen 12–18, THE HAGUE: *tel. 51.40.11*

Standing EEC Committee of the International Association of Soap and Detergent Industries:
32, rue Joseph II, BRUSSELS: *tel. 18.44.40*

European Committee for Ventilation and Drying Techniques:
10, Avenue Hoche, PARIS 8: *tel. MACmahon 38.00*

EEC Committee of the International Hairdressers' Association:
17, rue Notre-Dame-des-Victoires, PARIS 2: *tel. GUTenberg 38.24*

EEC Committee of the International Photograph and Cinema Traders Association (INTERPHOTO):
Neue Rabenstrasse 28, HAMBURG 36: *tel. 44.84.18*

European Union of the Advertising Industry:
112, rue de Trèves, BRUSSELS 4